100 days to Freedom

A Spiritual and Life Transformation Guide

By

Deacon Patrick Kearns

Dedication

100 days to Freedom is dedicated
to all those desiring to live a life of closeness and intimacy with Christ.
It is my sincere desire that this guide may help them in the same way
that it has helped me to transform my life.

+ Deacon Pat +

ISBN: 9781693690228

**Copyright 2019
Deacon Patrick Kearns
Sacramento, CA**

100 days to Freedom

+ Table of Contents +

Day		
-	Introduction and overview	Pg. 6
1	Personal weakness	Pg. 10
2	Making changes and new habits	Pg. 12
3	Turning failure into virtue	Pg. 14
4	Living outside of ourselves	Pg. 16
5	Holy Eucharist	Pg. 18
6	Struggle – The Saint Michael Prayer	Pg. 20
7	Mary – Our Mother too	Pg. 22
8	Adoration and time with Jesus	Pg. 24
9	Anxiety and fear	Pg. 26
10	Feeding our souls – Holy habits	Pg. 28
11	Setting Goals	Pg. 32
12	Authentic versus Integrity	Pg. 34
13	Never enough	Pg. 36
14	Review of disciplines	Pg. 38
15	Fasting	Pg. 40
16	Temptation and sin	Pg. 42
17	Gospel reflection	Pg. 44
18	Social media	Pg. 46
19	Forming our conscience	Pg. 48
20	Simplicity	Pg. 50
21	Motivation	Pg. 52
22	Morning prayer	Pg. 54
23	Our Fiat	Pg. 56
24	Routine	Pg. 58
25	Friendships/family	Pg. 60
26	Simple pleasures/delights	Pg. 62
27	Alcohol and concupiscence	Pg. 64
28	Review of disciplines	Pg. 66
29	Thinking and believing	Pg. 68
30	Thankfulness	Pg. 70
31	Life balance	Pg. 72
32	Knowing our path	Pg. 74
33	Creativity	Pg. 76
34	Lust and impurity	Pg. 78
35	Beatitudes	Pg. 80
36	Self-talk	Pg. 82
37	The Commandments	Pg. 84
38	The devil	Pg. 86
39	Humility	Pg. 88
40	The First Commandment – I am your God	Pg. 90
41	Core concepts	Pg. 92
42	Review of disciplines	Pg. 94
43	Fear of death – Faith brings Hope	Pg. 96
44	Mentoring	Pg. 98
45	Intellectual and personal growth	Pg. 100
46	Leaven	Pg. 102
47	The Angelus	Pg. 104
48	The Second Commandment – The Lord's name	Pg. 106
49	Intentional acts of kindness	Pg. 108

Day		
50	Mealtime prayers	Pg. 110
51	It is never too late	Pg. 112
52	Happiness	Pg. 114
53	How to live one's life	Pg. 116
54	The Third Commandment – Keep holy the sabbath	Pg. 118
55	Discernment	Pg. 120
56	Review of disciplines	Pg. 122
57	Clean on the inside	Pg. 124
58	Faith, hope, love, and death	Pg. 126
59	The Fourth Commandment – Honor thy mother and father	Pg. 128
60	Spiritual reading	Pg. 130
61	A focused purge	Pg. 132
62	Joyful service	Pg. 134
63	Retreats	Pg. 136
64	Be not afraid	Pg. 138
65	The Fifth Commandment - Thou shall not kill	Pg. 140
66	Trusting in God's providence	Pg. 142
67	The Rosary	Pg. 144
68	Littleness	Pg. 146
69	Mercy and forgiveness	Pg. 148
70	Review of disciplines	Pg. 150
71	The Sixth Commandment - You shall not commit adultery	Pg. 152
72	Walking	Pg. 154
73	Charism	Pg. 156
74	Cardinal Virtues	Pg. 158
75	Holy Marriage	Pg. 160
76	Community	Pg. 162
77	Stay awake	Pg. 164
78	Simplicity versus laziness	Pg. 166
79	The Seventh Commandment -Thou shall not steal	Pg. 168
80	Sleep	Pg. 170
81	Positive thinking	Pg. 172
82	A meal with friends	Pg. 174
83	Understanding suffering	Pg. 176
84	Review of disciplines	Pg. 178
85	A day of rest	Pg. 180
86	Catholic joy	Pg. 182
87	The Eighth Commandment- Thou shall not bear false witness	Pg. 184
88	Where is your Emmaus?	Pg. 186
89	Who is my neighbor?	Pg. 188
90	Mastering moderation	Pg. 190
91	Stewardship	Pg. 192
92	Temptation	Pg. 194
93	The Ninth Commandment- Thou shall not covet thy neighbor's wife	Pg. 196
94	Finding peace through obedience	Pg. 198
95	Dying to self	Pg. 200
96	Mary and Elizabeth show us the way	Pg. 202
97	Docility	Pg. 204
98	Review of disciplines	Pg. 206
99	The Tenth Commandment- Thou shall not covet thy neighbor's goods	Pg. 208
100	Living the *Life of Freedom*	Pg. 210
-	Appendix – Charts	Pg. 213

The Journey Begins

Introduction

The *100 days to Freedom* program was developed in response to an ever-growing desire of hundreds if not thousands of people wanting to escape from what they felt was a terminal downward spiral into darkness. The persistent attack from the powers of the world, the devil, and the fallen-self have left many with the feeling of being powerless over their developed sinful habits, their lack of prayerful ability, and their painful disconnect from God. So many have voiced that they had tried everything they knew to break the shackles of sinful vice but found their efforts to be ineffective. Consumed by their addictions they have come to realize that they were now at a place in their lives with a total loss of discipline and self-control.

The special design of the *100 days to Freedom* program, or way of life, offers a structured and wholistic approach, tried and tested, that includes spiritual, nutritional, and physical elements, as well as ample self-denial opportunities to build character, virtue, strengthen the body, heal the soul, nourish the mind, and most of all allows for a deeper connection to the spiritual world and especially with God.

The foundation of the program rests with the understanding that we are powerless without God, and that the answers to life will not be found from those of this world but rather from God himself. Additionally, to thrive we need to reconnect (or maybe connect for the first time) with God, and while developing an intimate relationship we will be able to identify the answers to those questions such as: Why am I here? What is my unique purpose? How do I make the right decisions? etc.

The spiritual element of the program includes attending daily Mass if possible, and if not possible, then establishing a formal prayer time, setting aside daily at least 30 minutes to include the prayerful reading of the daily Mass readings which can be obtained from various internet sites such as www.usccb.org, smartphone applications, and various books. The participant is also asked to pray a daily rosary knowing that the rosary is one of the most powerful weapons we have to fight against evil.

Free time should be used for spiritual reading that can be of the participant's choice such as the Bible, spiritual novels, books on the lives of the saints, early Church Fathers, etc. Each night there should be a formal examination of conscience where the participant reflects on the day's events, especially those events that could be considered blessings, temptations, and Godly encounters. During this examination, plans of action can be developed on how to deal with those negative circumstances if the same encounters present again in the future (such as dealing with repeated temptations). Efforts should be made for weekly adoration in front of the Blessed Sacrament, as well as monthly confession.

The physical element of the program will support a daily exercise routine of walking or running (depending on your degree of fitness). A routine of daily push-ups / sit-ups / lunges (or weight lifting), as well as daily stretches will be initiated but keep in mind that the participant will need to start slowly as the body becomes used to increased activity if the participant has been inactive for some time. Quantity is not as important as quality and routine, and the focus is to be on establishing the new habit of daily exercise.

The nutritional element of the program will focus on eating healthy and the building of a routine of self-denial and discipline. This will be accomplished by purging the body of empty calories and avoiding over-indulgence by eating 2-3 meals a day and no eating between meals. The participant will abstain from candy and desserts, avoid fast food, and develop a routine of fasting (maximum of 500 calories a day) on Mondays, Wednesdays, and Fridays. Fasting has been a long tradition in the spiritual/religious world for many reasons such as practicing discipline, strengthening the will, and developing confidence in the ability to overcome temptation. Fasting has also been shown in recent scientific evidence to have many physical healing and immune-strengthening properties as well. If one truly has a condition such as insulin-dependent diabetes or another medical condition that complicates the fasting element, then this discipline may be adjusted according to need. Additionally, one may want to consult their physician if they feel that this discipline might have questionable consequences. That said, without a clearly justified reason to forgo this discipline it should be adhered to. The fasting element has brought such great graces, insight, and rewards to so many that have completed the program. It is also the most cited element by those same participants who reported that the fasting discipline helping them profoundly with their transformation.

The final element of self-denial is an important aspect of the program that allows the participant to slowly build their mental and spiritual strength that will be beneficial in this spiritual formation/transformation. This self-denial also frees the participant from many timewasting habits and provides an opportunity to start feeding the mind and soul with holy and character/virtue building activities. This will be accomplished with the following guidelines: no major purchases (toiletries and needed items only), no watching of TV or movies, no use of social media, and no consumption of alcohol for the 100 days.

One exception to the program's discipline is Sundays. Sundays are days of celebration and should not be viewed as days of complete sacrifice. Sundays are opportunities to partake in a small relaxation of the program rules such as having ice cream with family or friends, watching a movie, or having a beer while enjoying a sports game on the TV. **Be Cautioned** – This day is to be a celebration of the resurrection of our Lord, and it is not an excuse for gluttony or succumbing to sinful temptation. These Sundays will be an exercise in temperance and are an important part of the program. In the beginning, one might choose to hold fast to the strictness of the program without relaxation, especially when one is dealing with an addiction, but by the later weeks of the program, the learning to deal with temptation and developing the skills of moderation and temperance will be important.

We are all unique and God works differently in each one of us, but often we come to a place in our lives where we know that it is the right time to make a sincere and important decision. We either turn toward God or we turn away. Often, we have turned away, yet we now have an opportunity to turn back toward Him and to learn new skills to keep us from turning away again in the future. *100 days to Freedom* will allow us to make the changes we need to make in our lives, and maybe for the first time experience a deep and intimate relationship with God, Jesus, and the Holy Spirit like we have never experienced before.

In the appendix of this book, you will find a supply of checklists that are essential to working the program. The checklists are to be used throughout the duration of the program and will help guide you through working the disciplines. The lists will also help as a daily reminder to complete the tasks, as well as a reminder of some of the elements that might be easily forgotten such as: no eating between meals, no alcohol, no candy/desserts, no fast-food, no major purchase, no TV or movies, and no social media. The checklists will also be used throughout the program for self-evaluation of the progress you are making.

Many have asked for a clarification regarding the listening to the radio, MP3 players, smartphone playlists, and podcasts. They are permitted if they are uplifting and Christ-centered. Be cautioned against the negative effects of news programs as they can be problematic during the transformation. ☺

100 days to Freedom Overview

100 days to reconnect with God and disconnect from societal influence while establishing new healthy habits and purging the old negative ones.

Start Date: _____   *(100 days duration)*   End Date: _____

Spiritual
1. Daily Mass preferred
    a. If not possible then a formal Spiritual Communion with 30 min prayer time (See Spiritual Communion prayer on the checklist)
    b. Daily Mass Readings
2. Daily Rosary
3. Formal Examination of Conscience nightly with a review of:
    a. Blessings
    b. Temptations
    c. Godly encounters
    d. Plan of action for the next day (How to deal with repeated temptations)
4. Daily spiritual reading
    a. Bible or
    b. Early Church Fathers or
    c. Other books such as the lives of the saints, etc.
5. Weekly adoration in front of the Blessed Sacrament
6. Monthly confession

Physical
1. Walk or Run (depending on your degree of fitness) daily
2. Push-ups / sit-ups / lunges daily or weight lifting routine
3. Stretches daily
4. 7-8 hours sleep a night

Nutrition
1. 2-3 meals a day - No eating between meals
2. No candy/desserts
3. No fast-food
4. Fasting (Maximum of 500 calories) Mon / Wed / Friday   *[may be adjusted for medical reasons]*

Self-Denial
1. No major purchases (Toiletries and needed items only)
2. No TV or movies
3. No social media
4. No alcohol

Day 1

Now that you have read the Introduction, the Program Overview, and looked at the checklist, you are ready to begin.

STOP!

Before you go any further, we must remind ourselves that we have no power, no discipline, no talents, and no abilities without God. This might seem a little bizarre to read or even to think, probably because the world showers us with the lie that we are powerful, smart, talented, and can do anything we set our minds to do all on our own. Lie, Lie, Lie!

Personal weakness is not something to be ashamed of, but rather a reminder that there is something much greater than ourselves. As Saint Paul states in relation to the thorn in his side that many scholars attribute to personal weakness and habitual sin, "Three times I begged the Lord about this, that it might leave me, but He said to me, 'My grace is sufficient for you, for power is made perfect in weakness.' I will rather boast most gladly of my weaknesses, in order that the power of Christ may dwell within me."

Let's begin in prayer:

Almighty God,
I am about to begin a journey that I know I will not be able to finish
if it were not for Your grace bestowed upon me.
I humbly ask that You help me every step of the way to follow the guidelines of this program and help me
to repent for my sinful ways and to grow closer to You who is all holy and powerful.
I ask that in my doubt, You give me hope.
I ask that in my fear, You give me confidence.
I ask that in weakness, You give me strength.
Above all things I desire to grow closer in intimate relationship with You

and that Your love will fill my heart and soul and that I can be an earthly reflection of You. Please bless my journey, Lord, and remain always near to me.

Amen.

Use this section below to journal any thoughts or inspirations from the meditation to help with further reflection.

Day 2

It has been said that the hardest part of making a change in one's life is taking the first step toward change. Congratulations, you have begun the process of change. With the absence of TV, movies, social media, alcohol, and eating between meals you probably felt very usual yesterday. Many have reported that when they started this program they felt a great deal of anxiety not knowing what to do with their time. Others have reported that they slept more in the first few days of the program than they had in years since they had nothing to distract them or to fill their free hours. Sleep is good. So many of us do not get enough sleep. Many experts have recommended that we need to sleep at least 6-8 hours a night consistently while also adhering to a set pattern of sleep such as a regular bedtime of 10 p.m. and awakening each morning consistently at 6 a.m. Part of this program is to be intentional about your sleep. Make a conscious decision to set a routine sleep pattern.

Over the next few days, start thinking about what new habits you wish to establish with what will feel like an abundance of free time. Some suggestions might be reading novels of the saints. One popular author is Louis de Wohl who brings the saints to life with his creative writing, or maybe with some of the writings of Bud Macfarlane or Michael O'Brien. You might want to begin some projects such as reorganizing the garage, redesigning the closet, building a shed, painting a room, planting a garden, etc. Innately we will want to fill our time with something. Being proactive and thinking about what would be healthy, holy, productive, and fulfilling can be the first step toward creating new habits and a new way of life. Our actions in life become a driving force of who we are and what we will become. Do not miss this opportunity to make thoughtful and intentional decisions about what type of new habits and hobbies you might enjoy in your life. Remember, what we feed our minds ultimately affects who we are in the long-term.

Let us pray,

Dear Lord,

I am thankful that you have enabled me to see that there is more to life than I currently know.

Although I do not have all the answers as of yet, I do trust in You.

Help me to trust even greater as I begin to develop my relationship with you in a more meaningful way.

Help me to be patient, calm, and optimistic about the future.

I also ask that you help me with ideas of ways to fill my newly obtained free time and that you will assist me with developing new healthy and holy habits.

Amen.

Use this section below to journal any thoughts or inspirations from the meditation to help with further reflection.

Day 3

Congratulations, you made it through days one and two, or maybe you don't think you had. It is very common to have started out with high hopes and then to not have completed even half of the tasks on the checklist. Do not fear! Today is a new day. The devil would love for you to throw in the towel before you have even gotten started. Remember Saint Paul, "I will rather boast most gladly of my weaknesses, in order that the power of Christ may dwell with me." By now you are probably getting the point. We are not relying on ourselves for this program to be successful, we are relying on God to work within us. When we find ourselves tired, weak, pessimistic, anxious, tempted, lazy-felling, etc., it isn't us we turn to, but rather we turn to God. That is what we call prayer. That is what we call turning to our Friend, to the one who knows us even better than we know ourselves. Don't forget, it is He who created you and He who knows what you truly need. He often uses our failures to implant within us an ever-stronger desire to not fail again. Let us not forget, He gave us a free will to make choices in life. Yes, He desires us to make good and holy choices, but even when we choose the contrary, He uses that decision or action to help us to grow in virtue.

Let's start to think of our weaknesses and failures in a new way, the way God might think of them. If our sin, our weakness, or our failings have to do with a particular root cause such as pride, greed, lust, or envy, know that God is probably trying to develop within you the character or virtue opposite of the root cause. The opposite of pride would be humility. If you struggle with laziness, God is probably wanting you to develop the virtue of perseverance. If you struggle with lust, maybe he wants you to develop a deeper selfless love within you. If it is greed, then maybe it is charity. You get the point. Take a minute and think about your failings in life. What is at its root? What is the opposite that maybe God is giving you the opportunity to develop? Remember, He is constantly trying to help us develop virtue and character in our lives, even by using our faults and bad decisions.

Let us pray,

Dear Lord,

I ask in a very personal way that You enter into my heart and my mind

and remind me just how much You love me.

I ask that You give me the strength to find peace and comfort in working my program today and that You will help me to see a piece of my beautiful uniqueness in the same way that You see me.

I can see all my faults and failures, as You see as well,

but help me to see Your love for me in a deep and meaningful way.

I am weak without You, please strengthen me so I may become fully the person You created me to be.

Amen.

Look at your checklist from yesterday. If you checked all the boxes, Congratulations! You are off to a great start. If there are many holes in the checklist do not despair. Set a goal today to check one more box than yesterday and ask for God's help. If you find yourself struggling to fit in all the elements of the program then focus on the spiritual elements since it is those that will empower the others, especially the rosary and the nightly examination of conscience.

Use this section below to journal any thoughts or inspirations from the meditation to help with further reflection.

Day 4

Welcome to day 4. Day by day you might begin to experience a slight shifting in your thoughts, behaviors, and your mood. Now that you are directing your thoughts and prayers to someone much greater than yourself and focusing your attention outward and not on your own personal needs by embracing self-denial, you will probably be more observant of those around you. Many have reported that as soon as they began the process of self-denial by fasting, giving up alcohol, abstaining from social media, and some of the other aspects of the program, they noticed that they were much more present to those around them. Funny how when we stop looking at ourselves, we can begin to see others more clearly.

Being less self-focused allows us to be more focused on the world around us. God often places people and situations in our path for a specific purpose. Our old selves would have probably missed nine out of ten of those Godly encounters without ever knowing it due to our self-preoccupation.

Today is a good day to work, or do your chores, or visit with family and friends, or talk to your neighbors all while looking for God's spirit in those encounters. Remember, God either wills things to happen or allows things to happen for a greater good. If we keep our eyes and hearts open, we will often see something deeper in the seemingly routine encounters of our lives. Look at that co-worker who shared something a little more personal than usual as someone who might be reaching out for comfort, love, or forgiveness. Look at that person who seemed to be driving erratically as someone who is probably going through a major life crisis and could use your prayers. Look at the untalkative woman at the checkout counter as someone who might have just lost her mother to cancer, her only friend in the world.

Beginning to live outside of ourselves opens a whole world of empathy, kindness, understanding, humility, and healing forgiveness. This way of thinking not only brings peace to ourselves and to others but allows us to be a reflection of God to the world. It is in that reflection that many can come to know who God is maybe for the first time and as we witness their reaction to our kindness and understanding we can also gain a deeper understanding of who God is to us as well.

Let us pray,

Loving God,
Help me today to be a person who loves others more than myself.
Help me to give more than I take.
Help me to fill my heart and my mind with such good thoughts of others that it radiates from my being.
Lord, help me with my self-denial and when I hunger, or thirst, or feel bored, or feel lonely,
help me to offer those thoughts and feelings as my sacrifice for all the times
when I have been selfish, self-serving, stubborn, prideful, and mean.
I love you Lord and I know that You love me.
Help me to feel loved and to be a loving presence to others.
Amen.

Use this section below to journal any thoughts or inspirations from the meditation to help with further reflection.

_____
_____
_____
_____
_____
_____
_____
_____
_____
_____
_____
_____

Day 5

Many Catholics find themselves either taking the Holy Eucharist for granted or maybe have never known the real significance of it. In the Gospel of John (6:52-59) we can learn from Jesus what his intentions were directly from the source:

The Jews quarreled among themselves, saying, "How can this man give us his flesh to eat?" Jesus said to them, "Amen, amen, I say to you unless you eat the flesh of the Son of Man and drink his blood, you do not have life within you. Whoever eats my Flesh and drinks my Blood has eternal life, and I will raise him on the last day. For my Flesh is true food, and my blood is true drink. Whoever eats my Flesh and drinks my Blood remains in me and I in him. Just as the living Father sent me and I have life because of the Father, so also the one who feeds on me will have life because of me. This is the bread that came down from heaven. Unlike your ancestors who ate and still died, whoever eats this bread will live forever." These things he said while teaching in the synagogue in Capernaum.

The question we should probably ask ourselves is, "What are my thoughts about the Holy Eucharist? Do I believe as the Church teaches, that it is the real presence of God (Jesus), body, blood, soul, and divinity? If not, why not? The early Christians believed it to be and many even gave their lives for that belief. Throughout the New Testament, Jesus clearly states what his intention was about the Holy Eucharist of which we just read one example. If I do believe that the Holy Eucharist is the true body, blood, soul, and divinity of Jesus Christ then ask yourself, "Do I worthily receive him? Do I value what that encounter is? Does that encounter reflect the honor, intimacy, and holiness of such an event? Have I cleansed my body before receiving God, prior to receiving Him in the Holy Eucharist, by removing all the mortal sin from my body through the use of Confession?"

The Holy Mass, which at its highest point, focuses on the Holy Eucharist and is recognized as the source and summit of our lives. The source and summit, that is our Catholic belief. Let's ask ourselves, have we made the Holy Mass and the Eucharist the source and summit of our lives, or is it just a part of our lives? Everything in life comes from our Creator and there is nothing greater in life than an encounter with the Creator, and that encounter occurs at every Mass. Is this what you believe, if not, why?

The next time you go to Holy Mass ensure that your soul is prepared for that encounter and that you open your eyes, heart, and mind to the miracle that occurs at every Mass. The miracle of Jesus becoming present in our midst.

Let us pray,

Oh, Holy One, Oh, Mighty One, I believe in you and help me with my unbelief.
Help me to experience the reality of what you have given to me
in the mystery of the Holy Eucharist.
Help me to understand what that means to be the source and summit of my life.
Help me to begin to live from Mass to Mass knowing that my life originates in the Mass,
is elevated to its highest point within the Mass, and that there is nothing greater
or more remarkable about my life than what occurs within the Mass.
Amen.

There is a book written by Dr. Scott Hahn by the name of *The Lambs Supper* that gives remarkable insight into what occurs within the Mass from a spiritual perspective. There are numerous things occurring symbolically and mysteriously at the Mass that if you had never been told or shown what they represent you would be unaware of so much beauty and grace. Many have reported that after reading that book, they instantly began to experience the Mass in a deeper, more profound, more fulfilling, and a much more enjoyable way.

Use this section below to journal any thoughts or inspirations from the meditation to help with further reflection.

_____

_____

_____

_____

_____

Day 6

By now you have settled into the program and are either doing a rock-solid job with complying with the regimen or find that you are struggling with some of the requirements. Either way is fine. This is a journey and not a test. There is no passing or failing grade, just a journey toward the truth. If you are doing well, be thankful, but not prideful. It is due to God's grace that you are doing well, not your own powers. Be careful, the devil will use your success to give you a false sense of powerfulness and pride and set you up for an even greater trap. If you are struggling to know that God has desired for you to struggle, it is part of His plan to draw you closer to Him in your powerlessness. Perseverance is a virtue that God desires for all Christians to possess, yet to develop that virtue we need to have things in our lives to struggle against. It is in the struggle that we can develop virtuous strength. The Saint Michael prayer is a great weapon to use and to pray in those times of weakness and temptation. Let us pray this prayer now and every day:

Saint Michael the Archangel, defend us in battle, be our protection against the wickedness and snares of the devil. May God rebuke him we humbly pray; and do thou, O Prince of the Heavenly host, by the power of God, cast into hell Satan and all evil spirits who prowl through the world seeking the ruin of souls.

Amen.

If you have not memorized this prayer do so today. It is not difficult and can easily be done in a day. Once memorized this is a powerful weapon that the devil will hate and can be an available tool carried with you at all times for your protection.

100 days to Freedom

Use this section below to journal any thoughts or inspirations from the meditation to help with further reflection.

Day 7

You have made it to day 7, congratulations. The most difficult part of every journey is taking the first step. You have not only begun this journey toward health, healing, and freedom, but you have endured an entire week. Give thanks to God for the graces he has bestowed on you so far, even if you think you have only been partially successful. **Warning** - Be prepared for an enhanced effort from the devil to attack you. He has no desire for you to be successful in this program or to grow closer in relationship to God.

Let us now turn our attention to the holiest human to have ever lived on earth (with the exception to Jesus in his human state), and to the one who's desire is to always direct us toward her son. We turn to Mary not only in our prayers of the holy rosary but in our thoughts and requests for her intercession. Mary is a powerful and comforting person who we can turn to in our times of weakness and struggle. In her motherly way, she will tenderly console us while at the same time advocate for us by delivering our prayers and requests directly to her Son. Let us not forget, at the time of His earthly death He made it clear that He was handing his mother over to us to be our mother as well.

Standing by the cross of Jesus were his mother and his mother's sister, Mary the wife of Clopas, and Mary of Magdala. When Jesus saw his mother - and the disciple there whom he loved, he said to his mother, "Woman, behold, your son." Then he said to the disciple, "Behold, your mother." And from that hour the disciple took her into his home. (John 19: 25-27)

Let us continue to develop a deeper understanding of and relationship with the mother of God (Jesus) and try to talk to her daily in our thoughts and prayers and then listen for her to respond in the quiet of our hearts.

Let us pray,

Hail, Holy Queen, Mother of Mercy, our life, our sweetness, and our hope! To thee do we cry, poor banished children of Eve. To thee do we send up our sighs, mourning and weeping in this valley of tears! Turn, then, O most gracious Advocate, thine eyes of mercy toward us, and after this, our exile, show unto us the blessed fruit of thy womb, Jesus.

O clement, O loving, O sweet Virgin Mary.

Pray for us, O holy Mother of God.
That we may be made worthy of the promises of Christ.

Amen.

Use this section below to journal any thoughts or inspirations from the meditation to help with further reflection.

Day 8

Time with Jesus is what will heal us, inspire us, give us reassurance, provide direction in our lives, and so much more. Remember, He is God, and God is the creator of everything. He is truth. He is love. We so often look to the world for comfort, recognition, inspiration, love, support, and direction. Yet, if we are seeking truth, wisdom, comfort, and acknowledgment, shouldn't we be turning toward the One who is all those things and the creator of all those things? Starting a routine of weekly adoration in front of the Eucharist will enable us to encounter Christ in a very personal way. Some parishes have perpetual adoration in an adoration chapel, while others only offer this periodically. Nevertheless, all parishes have a tabernacle. The only difference between the two is that Jesus is exposed in the adoration chapels instead of being secured inside the tabernacle. He is still present either way in his body, blood, soul, and divinity. Spending time with Him will allow us to not only get to know Him better, but it will also help us to get to know ourselves better. Being in the presence of truth has a special effect on us in the sense that things seem to look a little different and often are more easily put into perspective. Being in His presence can bring such clarity to so many confusing situations, thoughts, and decisions. The more time you spend with Him the deeper the relationship will become and the more graces and blessings you shall receive. Start this week a routine of spending some personal time with our Lord and Savior, at least for a few minutes if not an hour once a week.

Let us pray,

Blessed be God.
Blessed be His Holy Name.
Blessed be Jesus Christ, true God, and true Man.
Blessed be the Name of Jesus.

Blessed be His Most Sacred Heart.

Blessed be His Most Precious Blood.

Blessed be Jesus in the Most Holy Sacrament of the Altar.

Blessed be the Holy Spirit, the Paraclete.

Blessed be the great Mother of God, Mary most Holy.

Blessed be her Holy and Immaculate Conception.

Blessed be her Glorious Assumption.

Blessed be the name of Mary, Virgin, and Mother.

Blessed be St. Joseph, her most chaste spouse.

Blessed be God in His Angels and in His Saints.

Amen.

May the heart of Jesus, in the Most Blessed Sacrament, be praised, adored, and loved with grateful affection, at every moment, in all the tabernacles of the world, even to the end of time.

Amen.

Use this section below to journal any thoughts or inspirations from the meditation to help with further reflection.

Day 9

Anxiety and Fear, we all experience these emotions and mental states. It is the reason why so many of us struggle with overeating, alcoholism, and other vices. These vices bring comfort to our anxiety and fear, yet that comfort is only temporary and does nothing to resolve the underlying cause. These vices often lead to increased anxiety and fear over time because they often create additional problems. We need to find new alternatives to help us deal with our anxieties and fear. If we don't have other options, we will resort to what we know, our vices. The first step is to identify what our anxiety and fear look like. We must be able to identify how this is expressed in our unique way. Without the identification, we will struggle with the implementation of our action plan and we will be back to using our vices before we even know what has happened. Begin to identify what your mental and physical state is like just as you are being tempted to turn back toward your vice. That is what your anxiety and fear state look and feel like. Now think of a plan, what will you use and do to replace the use of your previous vice, will it be prayer, exercise, distraction, what will it be? Once you have developed a plan, begin to use it. My suggestion would be a combination of prayer and something else. The more you combat your fear and anxiety with a plan of action the better you will get at it.

Let us pray,

Dear Lord,
At times I find myself struggling with worries.
I know this is not Your will and that You wish me to lay my burdens at Your feet.
I know I can turn my cares over to You, who have died on the cross to set me free.
I choose to trust in You, Lord, to focus on You, and to leave behind my worries and my cares
as they are nothing in Your light.
When I find myself falling to my knees, let it be in front of You, with Your name on my lips, dear God.

100 days to Freedom

You will ease my burden and let me live free.

In Your Name,

Amen.

Use this section below to journal any thoughts or inspirations from the meditation to help with further reflection.

Day 10

"The Life of the body is the soul; the life of the soul is God" – Saint Anthony of Padua.

What is it that you do each morning to prepare for the day ahead? Do you focus on your physical needs, your spiritual needs, or your emotional needs? Or is it a blend? Saint Anthony reminds us that it is the soul that brings our body to life and that it is God that feeds our soul. Don't we all want to feel alive? Yet why do so many feel as if they are dead, or at least dead inside a shell? That is a common complaint with people suffering from depression or going through the dark night of the soul. Could it be that they had stopped feeding their soul and that has resulted in a progressive loss of life within them?

What is your daily morning routine? Does it include feeding the soul? Do you pray, read Scripture, listen to Christian podcasts? How is it that you are feeding your soul to not only prepare for the day ahead but to be strengthened by God? Take a few minutes and think about your holy habits or lack of holy habits. This program encourages daily Mass but if you are not able to attend then it is replaced with reading the daily Scripture, making a Spiritual Communion, and then allowing 30 minutes of meditative / prayer time to talk to and to listen to God. It also includes praying the rosary, a time to meditate upon the mysteries of Christ's life and to allow those events to bring deeper meaning and understanding to our life. We should also be reading some sort of spiritual reading to educate ourselves, inspire us with examples of holy people, and to gain greater insight into life. There is also the time of weekly adoration where we present ourselves to Christ and then bask in his holy presence. What we feed our minds, body, and soul become the food that not only nourishes and heals, but overtime has the greatest influence on what we will become.

There are many special prayers to choose from to help inspire our prayer life, but many have found that praying St. Patrick's Breastplate (also known as *The Cry of the Deer*) each morning helps feed their soul in a powerful and meaningful way.

Let us pray,

*I arise today
Through a mighty strength, the invocation of the Trinity,
Through belief in the Threeness,
Through confession of the Oneness
of the Creator of creation.*

*I arise today
Through the strength of Christ's birth with His baptism,
Through the strength of His crucifixion with His burial,
Through the strength of His resurrection with His ascension,
Through the strength of His descent for the judgment of doom.*

*I arise today
Through the strength of the love of cherubim,
In the obedience of angels,
In the service of archangels,
In the hope of resurrection to meet with reward,
In the prayers of patriarchs,
In the predictions of prophets,
In the preaching of apostles,
In the faith of confessors,
In the innocence of holy virgins,
In the deeds of righteous men.*

*I arise today, through
The strength of heaven,
The light of the sun,
The radiance of the moon,
The splendor of fire,
The speed of lightning,
The swiftness of wind,
The depth of the sea,
The stability of the earth,
The firmness of rock.*

*I arise today, through
God's strength to pilot me,
God's might to uphold me,
God's wisdom to guide me,
God's eye to look before me,
God's ear to hear me,*

God's word to speak for me,
God's hand to guard me,
God's shield to protect me,
God's host to save me
From snares of devils,
From temptation of vices,
From everyone who shall wish me ill,
afar and near.

I summon today
All these powers between me and those evils,
Against every cruel and merciless power
that may oppose my body and soul,
Against incantations of false prophets,
Against black laws of pagandom,
Against false laws of heretics,
Against craft of idolatry,
Against spells of witches and smiths and wizards,
Against every knowledge that corrupts man's body and soul;
Christ to shield me today
Against poison, against burning,
Against drowning, against wounding,
So that there may come to be an abundance of reward.

Christ with me,
Christ before me,
Christ behind me,
Christ in me,
Christ beneath me,
Christ above me,
Christ on my right,
Christ on my left,
Christ when I lie down,
Christ when I sit down,
Christ when I arise,

Christ in the heart of every man who thinks of me,
Christ in the mouth of everyone who speaks of me,
Christ in every eye that sees me,
Christ in every ear that hears me.

[Note that people sometimes pray a shorter version of this prayer just with these 15 lines about Christ above. The conclusion follows below.]

I arise today
Through a mighty strength, the invocation of the Trinity,
Through belief in the Threeness,
Through confession of the Oneness
of the Creator of creation.

Amen.

Use this section below to journal any thoughts or inspirations from the meditation to help with further reflection.

Day 11

So many of us set goals or expectations to only find that a short time later we missed the mark and then begin a downward spiral. The idea of failing can be devastating and can evaporate our motivations. Maybe there is a better way regarding the setting of goals and that has to do with living what is called life sprints. The idea is that goals should be small incremental achievements that allow for periods of a break in between. An example would be in weight loss. Instead of looking at the entire goal of losing 100 pounds, one could set a health sprint goal of losing five pounds. That means that you can make a life change (exercise, fewer calories, etc.) in order to lose five pounds. Then you relax a little, not to the extent that you were when you gained the weight, but relax some and then you can cruise for a while at that state. When you feel motivated and energized again, no minimum time requirement, you can begin another health sprint in order to lose another five pounds and then you can relax again and cruise until you are ready for another sprint. The idea is that it isn't a temporary diet, it is a gradual change in a person's habits. This same model can be used for many other things in life. How about a spiritual sprint? Maybe with a goal of attending daily Mass for one week and then backing off for a while until you feel motivated to try it again. This is surely different than saying I will go to daily Mass from now on. What about spiritual reading? How about saying I am going to read for 30 minutes a night every day this week and then take a pause until I feel motivated to do it again. You get the idea. We can use this model of living life one sprint at a time while trying to not fall back to where we began. Each sprint will gradually bring us to where we want to be without the feeling of failure. Why not give it a try?

Let us pray,

Dear Lord,
You made me for good works.
You gave me the desire to always learn and grow in my ability to love You and my neighbors.

Help me to make progress on my goals each day and not to worry about the conclusion

that You may bring out of that obedience.

Remind me regularly that Your conclusions of every matter will always bring fruit

even though the conclusion may be different than I was thinking.

Your ways are above my ways.

In Jesus' Name,

Amen.

Use this section below to journal any thoughts or inspirations from the meditation to help with further reflection.

Day 12

Authentic versus Integrity

Currently, in our modern culture, the word "Authentic" is in vogue. Everywhere you turn you hear just how authentic that person is and how we should all strive to be our authentic selves. But what does that mean, and is that truly a good thing? It appears that being authentic means that you are transparent, that what you see is what you get. That you are not putting up a facade, but rather exposing who you truly are without disguises or gimmicks. But being authentic doesn't mean you are a good person, it just means that you are aware of what you are and that you are alright with that. So, in theory, if you are a liar, a thief, an adulterer, and you don't try to hide it, you are authentic. Being authentic has nothing to do with having integrity. Integrity means that you are a person with the quality of being honest and have strong moral principles and that those principles guide your life. As Christians, we acquire our understanding of morality from the Creator of the world, the Creator of humanity, and the Creator of us. That person is God. God has revealed Himself in the most perfect way through his Son Jesus Christ, but even before He sent his Son, He gave us the Ten Commandments for our guide of what is moral and just:

1. I am the Lord thy God, thou shalt not have any strange gods before Me.
2. Thou shalt not take the name of the Lord thy God in vain.
3. Remember to keep holy the Sabbath day.
4. Honor thy father and mother.
5. Thou shalt not kill.
6. Thou shalt not commit adultery.
7. Thou shalt not steal.
8. Thou shalt not bear false witness against thy neighbor.
9. Thou shalt not covet thy neighbor's wife.
10. Thou shalt not covet thy neighbor's goods.

100 days to Freedom

Take a minute and reflect upon these Commandments and discern if you are an authentic person, or an authentic person with integrity, or neither.

Let us pray,

Loving and most gracious God,
We surrender our will to You today with the hope that You will instill within us
a greater desire to be a person of integrity.
We humbly ask that you open our eyes to see clearly our faults and that you give us the courage
to fight against temptation and to grow in holiness.
Help us to see the world around us as You see the world.
Help us to grow in patience, forgiveness, and faith.
It is with this faith that I will be filled with hope.
Hope for an even better tomorrow and a hope that
I will experience You even more profoundly in my life.
It is in that experience that I will grow in authenticity,
an authenticity that is grounded in Christian integrity.
Amen.

Use this section below to journal any thoughts or inspirations from the meditation to help with further reflection.

_____
_____
_____
_____
_____
_____
_____
_____
_____

Day 13

Never Enough

For many who have struggled with addiction they can relate to the term "Never Enough" because they have lived the reality that while trying to feed their addiction they were never completely satisfied, it was never enough. But never enough of what? The addiction or the vice might have been alcohol, food, or gambling. It might have been shopping or buying things excessively. Maybe it was pornography, sex, masturbation, or drugs. Maybe it was binging on movies. There are so many vices that one may turn to in our world. But for those who have struggled with addictions or the use of a sinful vice of some sort (Honestly don't we all fall into this category?) we have come to realize that whatever we were doing wasn't doing what we needed it to do. What was it that we were hoping to obtain? Maybe it was a greater peacefulness? Maybe a greater satisfaction in life? Maybe security, less anxiety, a sense of wholeness or completeness? Maybe to feel loved, or were we escaping the feeling of not being loved? Nevertheless, the more we used our addictions, or the vices in our lives, the more we were drawn away from what we truly desired.

So, where do we turn then if the use of these vices didn't work? The answer is quite simple. As Christians, we ask ourselves, who is it that represents what we are searching for? Who is it that is peacefulness, truth, wisdom, love, compassion, forgiveness, and honesty? The answer is God, of course, manifested in the Trinity: Father, Son, and Holy Spirit. The main focal point of this program is to connect (or reconnect) with God and to establish an intimate relationship with Him. As we work the program, increasing our prayer life, denying ourselves from bodily temptations, feeding our minds and body with things free of corruption, and reflecting on God's action in our lives, we gain the graces needed to start filling those areas of our lives that have seemed so empty. If we seek to find the answers in life that will make us whole and complete from people and things of this world it will never be enough, but if we seek to find those answers from God and godly things then the desire for vice and addiction in our lives will diminish as we live in the truth and love of our Creator.

Let us pray,

God of life,
You made me in Your perfect image, to live in Your love and to give You glory, honor, and praise.
Open my heart to Your healing power.
Come, Lord Jesus, calm my soul just as you whispered 'Peace' to the stormy sea.
St. Jude, most holy Apostle, in my need I reach out to you.
I beg you to intercede for me that I may find strength to overcome my use of vice in my life.
Bless all those who struggle with addiction.
Touch them, heal them, and reassure them of the Father's constant love.
Remain at my side, St. Jude, to chase away all evil temptations, fears, and doubts.
May the quiet assurance of Your loving presence illuminate the darkness in my heart
and bring lasting peace.
Amen.

Use this section below to journal any thoughts or inspirations from the meditation to help with further reflection.

_____

_____

_____

_____

_____

_____

_____

_____

_____

_____

Day 14

Congratulations, you have made it to day 14. This is a good time to stop, take a deep breath, and to evaluate how well, or maybe how not so well, the disciplines are going. Please take a minute, break out a pen or pencil, and complete this very important self-evaluation regarding adherence.

Spiritual	1 No Action	2 Almost none	3 Hit and miss	4 Almost perfect	5 Nailed it!
Daily Mass or Daily Mass readings and Spiritual Communion					
Daily Rosary					
Formal Examination of Conscience nightly					
Daily Spiritual reading					
Weekly adoration in front of the Blessed Sacrament					
Monthly Confession					

Physical	1 No Action	2 Almost none	3 Hit and miss	4 Almost perfect	5 Nailed it!
Walk or Run daily					
Push-ups / Sit-ups / Lunges daily or weight lifting					
Stretches daily					
7-8 hours' sleep a night					

Nutrition	1 No Action	2 Almost none	3 Hit and miss	4 Almost perfect	5 Nailed it!
2-3 meals a day - No eating between meals					
No candy / desserts					
No fast-food					
Fasting on Mon / Wed / Friday					

Self-Denial	1 No Action	2 Almost none	3 Hit and miss	4 Almost perfect	5 Nailed it!
No major purchases (Toiletries and needed items only)					
No TV or movies					
No social media					
No Alcohol					

Well, how did you do? Let me guess, maybe less than perfect? Join the club, I have yet to meet the perfect human or the one who completed the entire *100 days to Freedom* program without missing a discipline even once. That makes you normal, human, and maybe a little less than a superhero. Yet, as Christians, we are called toward a path of perfection, a life of holiness, a life in which we journey closer and closer to God.

The structure of this program will allow each of us to grow, to grow in virtue, character, self-discipline, and in relationship with God. Reflect once again on the scores you gave yourself above and then on the categories: Spiritual Life, Physical Health, Nutritional Health, and Self-Discipline. If you identify an area where there is more opportunity for growth, then try to place a greater focus on that area for the next week.

We have all been created in God's image and likeness, and we have been created as unique individuals. No two journeys are alike, just like no two scorecards are exactly alike. God is working in us in the exact way He feels that He needs to work in us to help us to travel our unique journey. Let go and allow Him to drive this journey. Our part is to be open to His promptings and respond when He calls.

Keep up the good work and as you progress day-by-day be prepared to enjoy the rewards that God has ready for you. Whenever we turn our focus away from ourselves and upon the Lord, we begin to realize what freedom truly feels and looks like.

Let us pray,

Father, look upon our weakness and reach out to help us with Your loving power.
You redeem us and make us Your children in Christ.
Look upon us, give us true freedom and bring us to the inheritance You promised.
We ask this through our Lord Jesus Christ, Your Son,
who lives and reigns with You and the Holy Spirit,
one God, forever and ever. Amen.

Day 15

Fasting

By now you have had multiple days of the fasting experience with the Monday, Wednesday, and Friday schedule. You probably have developed certain thoughts about the discipline and might have already noticed some of the benefits. Clearly, there are significant spiritual as well as physical benefits from the practice.

The physical benefits of ADF (Alternate Day Fasting) continue to be studied and with each study there seem to be more and more benefits revealed such as increased energy levels, clearer mentation, reduced inflammation, improved digestion, etc. One of the recent studies also found the following scientific results:

- The participants had fluctuating downregulation of amino acids, in particular, the amino acid methionine. Amino acid restriction has been shown to cause lifespan extension.
- They had continuous upregulation of ketone bodies, even on non-fasting days. This has been shown to promote health in various contexts.
- They had reduced levels of sICAM-1, a marker linked to age-associated disease and inflammation.
- They had lowered levels of triiodothyronine without impaired thyroid gland function. Previously, lowered levels of this hormone have been linked to longevity in humans.
- They had lower levels of cholesterol.
- They had a reduction of lipotoxic android trunk fat mass—commonly known as belly fat.

(Journal of Cell Metabolism - Alternate Day Fasting Improves Physiological and Molecular Markers of Aging in Healthy, Non-obese Humans. Aug 27, 2019. https://doi.org/10.1016/j.cmet.2019.07.016)

The spiritual aspects of fasting can easily be traced back to the time of Jesus and have been traditionally foundational in the Christian life, "Man shall not live by bread alone, but by every word that proceeds from the mouth of God." (Matthew 4:4)

St. Thomas Aquinas identified three values in fasting; repression of one's concupiscence (strong or ardent desire) of the flesh, atonement for one's sins, and the disposing of oneself to higher things.

Additionally, some have also reported that the purpose of fasting is to help the soul turn back to God through the conversion of the heart and that we need to constantly ask the Spirit's help in teaching us how to fast as well as how to pray.

As we fast, we find that we are more alert to the workings of the Holy Spirit. By temporarily removing the usual and routine process of eating, and creating an internal void, we allow God a space in our hearts to act. Fasting and the effects bring about a reminder that we are hungry. By removing the food that superficially satisfies and satiates, we are directed to the spiritual realm and it is there that we discover just how unsatisfying the temporal life can be. It is there that we begin to realize what it is that God wants to feed us. When we detach from food, our senses often become sharper and we can better understand that God is the source of the only food that lasts forever. Isn't that what we are truly hungry for? Isn't that what we are craving?

"Prayer, mercy, and fasting: These three are one, and they give life to each other. Fasting is the soul of prayer; mercy is the lifeblood of fasting. Let no one try to separate them; they cannot be separated. If you have only one of them or not all together, you have nothing." Saint Peter Chrysologus (c. 380 – c. 450). As you embrace your days of fasting know that you fast is also your prayer and throughout the entire day you are praying to God.

Let us pray,

Hanging as a vine upon the Wood,

O Christ our Savior,

Thou hast made the ends of the earth to drink from the wine of incorruption.

Therefore do I cry aloud:

I am darkened always by the hateful drunkenness of sin;

Give me to drink from the sweet wine of true compunction,

and grant me now the strength, O Savior,

to fast from sensual pleasures,

for Thou art good and lovest mankind.

Amen.

(St. Joseph Studite, Lenten Triodion)

Day 16

Temptation and Sin

Have you ever wondered why we are so easily tempted and even the holiest of men and women still sin even when they try not to? Remember good old Saint Paul who expressed his frustration with just this situation, *"For what I am doing, I do not understand. For what I will to do, that I do not practice; but what I hate, that I do" (Romans 7:15)*. Isn't this just like us at times? When we are sinning, we often don't understand why we are doing it. And the things we know we should do we don't do them often enough. And for the things we know we should never do we still do them from time to time. Why is this so?

We have all heard of Adam and Eve and what we Christians call original sin. That is where it all began and our original parents passed something horrible onto us, concupiscence. To understand concupiscence, we must first understand a few things, especially regarding Adam and Eve. God created Adam and Eve and filled them with all the graces and virtue they would ever need, and they experienced a close relationship with God unlike our ability to understand. At the time there was no sin, no sickness, no suffering, and no death. Living in the Garden of Endon was a monumental utopia. When creating Adam and Eve God also instilled within them a free will. We all know what happens next, the devil tempted Eve to do what God asked her not to do, and Adam followed along. In that act of defiance, they separated themselves from God and lost their freedom, forgetting that it was God and his commands that produced true freedom in their lives.

Because of the unity of the human race, everyone is affected by the sin of our first parents, just as, in turn, humanity is restored to a right relationship with God by Jesus Christ. Original sin as it relates to everyone is not something we committed but rather contracted. It is a state rather than an act. It is this original sin that underlies all other sins and causes our natural powers of knowing and loving to be wounded. Because of it, we are subject to ignorance which makes it difficult for us to know the truth, and for some, even to believe that truth exists. We also endure suffering and death and have a disorder in our appetites and an inclination to sin. This inclination is called concupiscence.

So, what is the main result of original sin? By their sin, Adam and Eve, the first man and woman, our original parents, lost their original holiness and justice that they received from God, not only for themselves but for all human beings.

We must also understand that sin is not a weakness we can overcome by our own efforts. It is a condition from which we need to be saved. Jesus is our Savior. So now you understand why having a close and personal relationship with Christ is so important. I think most of us would agree that we are not even close to the holiness of Saint Paul. Yet Saint Paul could not withstand the effects of temptation without God's help. In maddening frustration, he cried out *"Miserable one that I am! Who will deliver me from this mortal body?" (Romans 7:24)* It was with this understanding that Saint Paul came to understand in his faith that, *"Where sin increased, grace overflowed all the more" (Romans 5:20)*.

A truth about humanity - No matter how sinful we human beings become, the desire for God never dies while we are on earth. No matter how holy we grow, the sting of evil always gnaws at us from the effects of original sin. So, when you feel that there is an inner turmoil battling within you, know that you are normal, you are human. We need Christ to save us from ourselves much of the time and that is why our prayer lives and the use of the Sacraments, especially the Sacrament of Reconciliation (Confession) is so important because it keeps our hearts and souls pure and open for the reception of grace into our lives.

Let us pray,

Father,
I know that I have broken Your laws and my sins have separated me from You.
I am truly sorry, and now I want to turn away from my past sinful life toward You.
Please forgive me and help me avoid sinning again.
I believe that Your Son, Jesus Christ died for my sins, was resurrected from the dead, and is alive.
Please send Your Holy Spirit to help me obey You, and to do Your will for the rest of my life.
Amen.

Day 17

Are we able to hear the truth when it is spoken? Do we act upon the truth with love and charity? Do we recognize men and women of God and do we listen to them?

Jesus said to the Pharisees: *"There was a rich man who dressed in purple garments and fine linen and dined sumptuously each day. And lying at his door was a poor man named Lazarus, covered with sores, who would gladly have eaten his fill of the scraps that fell from the rich man's table. Dogs even used to come and lick his sores. When the poor man died, he was carried away by angels to the bosom of Abraham. The rich man also died and was buried, and from the netherworld, where he was in torment, he raised his eyes and saw Abraham far off and Lazarus at his side. And he cried out, 'Father Abraham, have pity on me. Send Lazarus to dip the tip of his finger in water and cool my tongue, for I am suffering torment in these flames.' Abraham replied, 'My child, remember that you received what was good during your lifetime while Lazarus likewise received what was bad; but now he is comforted here, whereas you are tormented. Moreover, between us and you, a great chasm is established to prevent anyone from crossing who might wish to go from our side to yours or from your side to ours.' He said, 'Then I beg you, father, send him to my father's house, for I have five brothers, so that he may warn them, lest they too come to this place of torment.' But Abraham replied, 'They have Moses and the prophets. Let them listen to them.' He said, 'Oh no, father Abraham, but if someone from the dead goes to them, they will repent.' Then Abraham said, 'If they will not listen to Moses and the prophets, neither will they be persuaded if someone should rise from the dead.'"*

What does this Gospel message say to you? How can this be applied to your life? Do you ever feel that you can put off important things, or rationalize why they might not be as important as others might feel that they are? Is your motto why do today what can be done tomorrow? What if tomorrow never comes? Are you ready to be judged by God? Yes, God is merciful, but He is also just. Are you prepared for the justice of God?

Let us pray,

Holy Spirit, sweet guest of my soul,

abide in me and grant that I may ever abide in thee.

Holy Spirit, sweet guest of my soul,

abide in me and grant that I may ever abide in thee.

Holy Spirit, sweet guest of my soul,

abide in me and grant that I may ever abide in thee.

Use this section below to journal any thoughts or inspirations from the meditation to help with further reflection.

Day 18

Social Media, TV, and Movies

Now well into the program, you might be wondering about the discipline of no TV, movies, or social media. Why is this so important? Well, for many of us we have filled our lives with such distraction that we have no time for God. Every waking minute is filled with some sort of activity or external noise. With that constant and resonating noise, there is no chance to hear the subtle callings and inspirations of the Holy Spirit. It was once described that God speaks to us in the quiet of our hearts. Additionally, Jesus and His ways can often be thought of as Christ walking through our minds holding a candle. He strolls around between ideas and when he wants to illuminate one of those ideas, he holds the candle even closer to that idea, that potential inspiration, to brighten it and bring attention to it. It is very subtle and if our minds are bombarded with distractions, we will be oblivious to His action. Therefore, quiet is so important in our lives, to be able to hear God.

Another reason why we abstain from TV, movies and social media is because of the messages that they fill our minds with. I think we can all agree that those forms of media have been saturated with filth and immorality. The more we expose ourselves to this type of sinfulness the more desensitized we become and the devil loves that. The more that sin can be presented as good, and goodness portrayed as evil, the quicker our moral compass can be weakened and confused. The *100 days to Freedom* program allows the participants the opportunity to break away from their addictions to social media, movies, and TV, and the time spent on those vices to be replaced with things like spiritual reading, prayer, listening to uplifting podcasts, and wholesome and enjoyable hobbies.

Many participants of the program had not realized their degree of addiction to social media, the internet, and movies until they began this program and were asked to give them up for a period of time. It was then that they felt the constant powerful urge and pull to reengage. These are the same people who after a few weeks noticed the great freedom that they had obtained once detoxified from the habit. There are great forces of evil at work in our culture and these forces have used the available media to spin their web of deceit, to tempt, and to lure you away from a life of holiness, purity, and honor.

THE CHALLENGE - Take a moment to think about what you allow to influence your life, what it is that you are feeding your mind and soul? Use this new understanding as a wake-up call to be aware of how the world and the devil have been given access to your influential mind by the use of social media, TV, and movies.

Yes, there can be good in those things just mentioned, TV, social media, and movies, they are not completely bad and sinful. However, it takes great discernment, willpower, and moderation to be able to use them without being negatively influenced by them. To be able to gain those abilities we need to take a step back, withdraw from them for a time to see them for they truly are, and then make a decision for the future about how we will allow them back into our lives, how to moderate their use, and how to not be negatively affected by them.

Let us pray,

Almighty and most Merciful God,
graciously hearken unto our prayers;
and free our hearts from the temptations of evil thoughts;
that we may worthily become a fit habitation for Thy Holy Spirit.

Use this section below to journal any thoughts or inspirations from the meditation to help with further reflection.

Day 19

Forming Our Conscience

Many have said, "Let your conscience be your guide." Well, that can be good advice if one's conscience is well-formed. But what is a well-formed conscience? I like to think of it as what we often do in the medical field when it comes to helping patients make decisions about operations and even the use of certain medications. Both of those examples often have benefits as well as risks. The patient first needs to be educated by the treating physician who is knowledgeable in the benefits and risks of these choices and once the patient has the knowledge needed to make an appropriate decision, they can give their informed consent or non-consent. The keyword here is informed. We are like the patient in this example and Jesus is like our physician. We first need to be educated by Jesus regarding the things in life, often the truths in life, before we can make appropriate decisions and then have the ability to give and make informed decisions. One might ask how is it that we learn from Jesus? Well, there are Scriptures that we can access. There are the teachings of the Church that can easily be found in the Catechism of the Catholic Church. One may request time with a priest, deacon, sister, brother, or a wise spiritual person to learn about the faith or to request help with discernment. There are also various internet sites, podcasts, and media programs that are great tools to help with gaining a greater understanding of the ways of Christ.

One of the greatest travesties of our time is that so many people are making significant decisions in their lives, decisions that will have lasting effects without taking the time to thoroughly explore their potential options, especially in relation to their professed faith, and how each potential choice has certain consequences and rewards. Many who identify as Christians often do not take the time to consult the teachings of their faith before making their decisions and by not doing so, they make choices and decisions in direct contrast to their professed faith.

EXERCISE - Take a moment and reflect upon how you make decisions in your life, especially the larger decisions such as marriage, children, jobs, buying a house, having a relative move in with you, thoughts of donating or tithing, taking on causes, how you vote, etc. Do you first research what our Church teaches on these subjects? Have you consulted the Catechism, or Scripture, or spoken to a spiritual director/clergy?

An example of the process of informing our conscience regarding making big decisions could be as follows:

1. First, pray about the issue/decision choices and ask God to help you by giving you His grace and the ability to think wisely and prudently.
2. Involve others whom this decision might affect: spouse, children, friends, etc.
3. Turn to the Catechism and explore if there is a teaching of the Church that can help you.
4. Make a list of the pros and cons especially as it relates to you as a Christian and your Christian journey.
5. Ask the question, "Will this action/decision help me to grow closer to Christ or will it pull me away? Or is it neutral?"
6. Consult with a cleric (bishop, priest, deacon), or religious (sister or brother) or a wise spiritual guide.
7. Pray once again for God's guidance.

Let us pray,

Father,
I need the wisdom that only your Spirit can give me.
Help me to not lean solely on my own opinions, thoughts, or dreams —
or what my society, culture, and those around me have to say.
I need godly — not earthly — wisdom, Lord.
Please supply me in knowledge and truth as I battle these tough decisions and uncertainty.
Father open my eyes to the barriers holding me back from spiritual progress and help me to walk confidently as I discern the next steps I need to take in my life.
Amen.

Day 20

Simplicity

"The splendor of the rose and the whiteness of the lily
do not rob the little violet of its scent nor the daisy of its simple charm.
If every tiny flower wanted to be a rose, spring would lose its loveliness."
— St. Therese of Lisieux

At the age of 14, on Christmas Eve in 1886, Therese had a conversion that transformed her life. From then on, her powerful energy and sensitive spirit were turned toward love, instead of keeping herself happy. At 15, she entered the Carmelite convent in Lisieux to give her whole life to God. She took the religious name Sister Therese of the Child Jesus and the Holy Face. Living a hidden, simple life of prayer, she was gifted with great intimacy with God. Through sickness and dark nights of doubt and fear, she remained faithful to God, rooted in His merciful love. After a long struggle with tuberculosis, she died on September 30, 1897, at the age of 24. Her last words were the story of her life: "My God, I love You!"

The world came to know Therese through her autobiography, "Story of a Soul". She described her life as a "little way of spiritual childhood." She lived each day with unshakable confidence in God's love. "What matters in life," she wrote, "is not great deeds, but great love." Therese lived and taught a spirituality of attending to everyone and everything well and with love. She believed that just as a child becomes enamored with what is before her, we should also have a childlike focus and totally attentive love. Therese's spirituality is of doing the ordinary, with extraordinary love.

She loved flowers and saw herself as the "little flower of Jesus," who gave glory to God by just being her beautiful little self among all the other flowers in God's garden. Because of this beautiful analogy, the title "little flower" remained with St. Therese.

Saint Therese was also declared a Doctor of the Church due to the powerful impact she has had on others with her little way and ideas of simplicity. A few of her quotes are as follows:

"Miss no single opportunity of making some small sacrifice, here by a smiling look, there by a kindly word; always doing the smallest right and doing it all for love."

— *St. Therese of Lisieux*

"For me, prayer is a surge of the heart; it is a simple look turned toward heaven, it is a cry of recognition and of love, embracing both trial and joy."
— *St. Therese of Lisieux*

"Holiness consists simply in doing God's will and being just what God wants us to be."
— *St. Thérèse de Lisieux*

"I know now that true charity consists in bearing all our neighbors' defects-- not being surprised at their weakness but edified at their smallest virtues."
— *St. Therese of Lisieux, Story of a Soul: The Autobiography of St. Therese of Lisieux*

Let us pray,

O Little Therese of the Child Jesus, please pick for me a rose
from the heavenly gardens and send it to me as a message of love.
O Little Flower of Jesus, ask God to grant the favors
I now place with confidence in your hands.

(mention in silence here your petition)

St. Therese, help me to always believe as you did in
God's great love for me, so that I might imitate your "Little Way" each day.
Amen.

Day 21

Motivation

Many people are in search of motivation and ask questions such as, "Where can I go or who can I see to motivate me?" It is true that we can turn to others for inspiration, often listening to their words, witnessing how they live their lives, and even looking at their accomplishments, but the source of motivation comes from within. If one is struggling with motivation, they often have neglected the most essential thing. To have the motivation to do something, to change something, or to achieve something a person should always begin with having a vision and a goal.

Developing a vision is to think about something in what is called a high-level view or a macro view. An example might be that a person creates a vision that they want to be healthy, happy, peaceful, energetic, and self-confident. Then they start to look at what they need to do to fulfill that vision. This usually means looking at and then planning the steps they will need to complete to reach periodic goals. Maybe call this the interventions or the actions. They can then develop a plan using those interventions or incremental actions to reach goals. By progressively setting goals and then reaching them there will be a progression in the direction of the vision and that vision can eventually become a reality.

After doing this and if one begins to struggle with their motivation, they can reflect on their vision and then at their plan of reaching that vision. Often, we need to scale down our goals so they aren't so farfetched and perceived to be out of immediate reach. It is better to have many smaller goals and fewer large ones. By having goals that are more frequently reachable we can see that we are making progress. It is in the progress that we will find additional motivation and will feel inspired to strive even harder.

EXERCISE – Think of a personal vision that you would like to see for yourself. Please write it down:

100 days to Freedom

_____

_____

What are some of the steps that you could do to make that vision a reality?

1. _____

2. _____

3. _____

4. _____

What would be some of the smaller goals that you could establish that would lead you to that vision?

1. _____

2. _____

3. _____

4. _____

Let us pray,

O good and gentle Jesus, hear my prayer!

Lift me up, Lord, and show me Your face.

Give me hope and grant me the grace to continue my journey

undisturbed by the troubled emotions that I may feel at times.

Give me an understanding of how You carried your own cross,

embracing it and carrying it out of love for me.

In your mercy, grant me the strength to push forward this way,

with love and acceptance.

Amen.

Day 22

Morning Prayer

It has become a habit for many people of faith to start their day with a prayer of thanksgiving, encouragement, and hope. After a restful night's sleep, free of many of the horrific things that occur under the shade of darkness of the nighttime hours, we can feel compelled to thank God for His protection and for our safety. If we awake and are free of horrific pain or debilitating illness, we can thank God for our health. If we have food in our cupboards and in our refrigerator, we may want to thank God for what he has provided for us. If we have been blessed with a spouse or someone who loves and cares for us, we can give our thanks for companionship. There are so many things that we can be thankful for if we allow ourselves to be aware of all that surrounds our lives. Now there are also things that may bring us anxiety and fear and the mornings might present these thoughts as well. The mornings are a good time to bring these issues up in our prayer while asking God to calm our hearts and to give us the wisdom and strength to deal with them. It is also a time to deeply reflect on why these things might be in our lives. Have they appeared due to something we have created, or are they unprovoked? What might be the lesson that God is trying to teach us through this experience? Prayers are often filled with great emotions, focused on thankfulness, laments, and requests. We can also include in our prayers the desires that we have for others. We can pray for our friends, our family, and even for those we don't personally know but we are aware they do exist in the world and are suffering. We can pray for those who have departed, especially for those that we think might still be in purgatory awaiting their complete purification before they transition into heaven. Those in purgatory are often the forgotten souls and they need our prayers desperately.

There are traditional ways to offer a morning prayer such as upon awakening, climbing out of bed and onto one's knees, making the sign of the cross, and then reciting a formal prayer such as,

> *"O Jesus, through the Immaculate Heart of Mary, I offer you my prayers, works, joys, sufferings of this day, in union with the Holy Sacrifice of the Mass throughout the world."*

And then adding some personal intentions. Or using one of the other of thousands of available traditional prayers as a template to structure your prayerful thoughts.

Bishops, priests, deacons, religious – and some laity if they so choose – all pray the Liturgy of the Hours, also known as the Divine Office, the official prayers of the Church beginning in the early morning and at set times throughout the day. These prayers are specific to each day and to each of the dedicated hours and are composed mostly of the Psalms, but also other scriptures and other spiritual writings. This unified prayer that spans every corner of the earth and across every time zone allows the Church to be in a constant state of prayer throughout the world with each individual praying for the entire human race.

However, prayer doesn't always have to be spoken. At times we have no words to express our thoughts and feelings, we need to just place ourselves into a prepared mental state allowing us to be present to God. In our thoughts, we can ask God to become present to us and then we may bask in that presence allowing God to speak to us if He so chooses, and in whatever way He may decide to communicate with us. Saint Therese said, "Frequently, only silence can express my prayer."

CHALLENGE – If not already doing so, begin a routine of starting each day, upon awakening, with a prayer directed to one of the Holy Trinity: God the Father, God the Son, or God the Holy Spirit. Include an aspect of thankfulness, ask for help when needed, and always include someone other than yourself in your prayers.

Let us pray,

> *In the Name of the Father, and of the Son, and of the Holy Spirit.*
> *Our Father, Who art in Heaven, hallowed be Thy Name.*
> *Thy Kingdom come. Thy Will be done, on earth, as it is in Heaven.*
> *Give us this day our daily bread and forgive us our trespasses as we*
> *forgive those who trespass against us, and lead us*
> *not into temptation, but deliver us from evil.*
> *In the Name of the Father, and of the Son, and of the Holy Spirit.*
> *Amen.*

Day 23

Our "Fiat"

"By pronouncing her "fiat" at the Annunciation and giving her consent to the Incarnation, Mary was already collaborating with the whole work her Son was to accomplish. She is mother wherever He is Savior and head of the Mystical Body" (Catechism of the Catholic Church # 973).

"Behold I am the handmaiden of the Lord. May it be done to me according to your Word" (Luke 1:38). This is Mary's "fiat," her "Yes" to the Lord.

"What came about in bodily form in Mary, the fullness of the godhead shining through Christ in the Blessed Virgin, takes place in a similar way in every soul that has been made pure. The Lord does not come in bodily form, for 'we no longer know Christ according to the flesh,' but He dwells in us spiritually and the Father takes up His abode with Him, the gospel tells us. In this way the child Jesus is born in each of us." - Gregory of Nyssa

We also have the opportunity to say "Yes" and give our fiat to our Lord. These opportunities begin with how we choose to live our lives. We have been given the Commandments. We have been taught the foundations of our faith, or are still learning them, and we have a choice to either fully engage in the Christian way of life, 'The Way,' or not. By the fact that we know God, He has called us to Himself and by using our free-will we have a choice in how we respond.

Let's be honest for a minute and ask ourselves this question, "Am I 100% responding to God by living in such a way as Jesus had modeled for us in His way of life, His teachings, and what He directed us to do?" If we are honest, most of us will respond with a semi-yes, a partial yes, and maybe even a resounding 'somewhat.' Well, is that what God is asking of us, to be a partial Christians, to be semi-convicted? You see where this is going. The *100 days to Freedom program* was developed in part to be a catalyst for not only making a change in our lives but to also teach us specific tools to be used to engage more fully in this Christian way of life and to provide an opportunity to self-reflect in a critical way to reveal our inadequacies. Once revealed, we can then deal with them and journey toward becoming the best version of ourselves that we can become and to grow into the person who God truly created us to be.

As men and women of faith, we are to be disciples of the One that we follow. For us Christians, we are to be disciples of Christ. We are to be disciplined in the ways of the teacher and progressively grow to fulfill what we have been taught. This is a process of conversion and this conversion begins with our own fiat. It comes as we say "Yes" not only in our words but in our actions. The more we say "Yes" to our Lord and to the opportunities that He places in our lives, the more we can become detached from ourselves and more closely attached to God. As we lose ourselves in God, we can find ourselves more completely in God and will be able to more clearly see God within ourselves.

EXERCISE –

What does it mean to be a Christian? _____

_____

_____

_____

_____

_____

Let us pray,

He ascended into Heaven, and sitteth at the right hand of God, the Father almighty; from thence He shall come to judge the living and the dead. I believe in the Holy Spirit, the holy Catholic Church, the communion of saints, the forgiveness of sins, the resurrection of the body and life everlasting.
Amen.

Day 24

Routine

It has now been well over three weeks since embarking on the *100 days to Freedom* journey and you have probably established a pattern or routine of completing some of the disciplines. As we develop routines of doing things, they slowly become habits. Doing something in the same way and at the same time of day for a specific amount of time will slowly turn that practice into a usual way of doing something and the usual way of living our lives. It will become second nature, and then we will complete that thing, or practice, without even thinking about it. A few examples might be praying the daily Mass readings while having your morning coffee. Or examining your conscience, viewing the events of the previous day in relation to God and your relationship with God, as you go for your morning walk. Also, praying your rosary each night at the time when you climb into bed. Maybe designating Thursday as your weekly holy hour day, the same day you have the car washed, as the day you swing by the church after work to spend an hour in front of Jesus in the tabernacle. And finally, what about assigning the first Saturday of each month, the same day as your monthly haircut, as your routine Confession day? By making these desired practices a part of our daily routine and associating them with other routines in our lives will help us to establish them as habits in our lives.

Three weeks is just a beginning and we will need much more time to solidify our newly acquired practices, turning them into solid habits. Please look at your program card and the disciplines on that card. Evaluate if you have established routines for those disciplines or if you are trying to squeeze them into your busy life? The goal would be to have those disciplines be the foundation of your life and that your life surrounds those disciplines. But, to begin, let's start with making them well-established routines in our lives and this can be done best by associating them with things that you have already made routines as mentioned above.

Let us pray,

O my God!

I offer Thee all my actions of this day for the intentions and for the glory of the Sacred Heart of Jesus. I desire to sanctify every beat of my heart, my every thought, my simplest works, by uniting them to Its infinite merits; and I wish to make reparation for my sins by casting them into the furnace of Its Merciful Love.

O my God! I ask thee for myself and for those whom I hold dear, the grace to fulfill perfectly Thy Holy Will, to accept for love of Thee the joys and sorrows of this passing life, so that we may one day be united together in Heaven for all Eternity.

Amen.

Use this section below to journal any thoughts or inspirations from the meditation to help with further reflection.

Day 25

Friendships

When a person possesses one or more good friends that they can stay connected with, interact with, and regularly share time together, they find that they do not have the tendency to feel isolated and alone. It is natural for many people as they go through the dark times of their lives, either struggling with a degree of depression – or more than likely just experiencing a natural progression of the spiritual journey called the Dark Night of the Spirit or the Soul – that they pull away from people. During these times of struggle, many people lose the desire to be around others. Yet, it is being around others if they are the kind of people who are supportive, loving, faithful, and kind, which will ultimately help them to get through those dark days.

Think about the people you have in your life. Do you have one or two people that you would consider as good friends? Do you regularly spend time with them? Do you interact with them at least one or two times a week? What about your family? Do you have brothers or sisters that you consider to be good and faithful people? Do you regularly spend time with them? Those in your family have an additional quality that at times the others do not. People from your family often know you better than most and not only can they offer added insight due to their familiarity with your life journey, but they probably love you and care for you deeply. Deepening relationships with the members of one's family can be beneficial in many ways, but especially as a companion in life as one grows in age. Brothers and sisters already have a unique bond through their shared experiences and can be a tremendous support in good times and bad.

God did not create us to be isolative and withdrawn. He created us to live amongst others and to befriend others. Yes, some of us are extroverts, and some introverts, yet that is not an excuse for the introverts to not connect with others and to share their lives with others. It just means that those introverts will need some time alone to recharge their batteries since being with others, even as good as that experience is, does drain them of the energies. That is not something extroverts need to be concerned about since the more time they spend around others the more energized or charged-up they become.

CHALLENGE – Make an effort to connect or reconnect with one or two people in your life that you discern will be a support, friend, companion, or confidant. Take a minute and first pray to God for insight and wisdom and then for His grace to overshadow your efforts. Keep in mind, our ways are not God's ways, and what we desire might not always be in the plan of God for you, but do not get discouraged since He (God) knows exactly what you need and when you need it.

Let us pray,

Guardian Angel, watch over those whose names you can read in my heart.
Guard over them with every care and make their way easy and their labors fruitful.
Dry their tears if they weep; sanctify their joys; raise their courage if they weaken; restore their hope if they lose heart, their health if they be ill, truth if they err, repentance if they fail.
Amen.

Use this section below to journal any thoughts or inspirations from the meditation to help with further reflection.

Day 26

Simple delights

Have you wondered why there is the discipline in the *100 days to Freedom* program of no major purchases? Some may have thought it has to do with self-denial. Others may have thought that it might have something to do with removing distractions. A few might have even considered that it has to do with removing excess from their lives. Well, they are all correct at least to some degree. By limiting the ability to spend money to just the necessities in life, like toilet paper, food, and toothpaste, one can quickly come to realize that it really doesn't take much to get by in life and to be content. We have the tendency to feel that we need a whole lot of things to get by in life when in all actuality we need very little to be comfortable. As you progress through the program, especially by the 30th or 45th-day mark, it becomes evident that a person doesn't need many external things to be happy and feel cared for. Typically, one needs food to eat, yet much less than what we had been accustomed to eating prior to participation in the program. We need clothing, shelter, and water. That is about it as it related to meeting our nutritional and safety needs.

Many past participants of the program have reported that they had no idea how much time and energy they exhausted chasing things that they felt were necessary for life to only find out during the program that those things were not necessary at all. Life can be very simple and with that simplicity can also bring simple delights. For one who regularly fasts, has developed the habit of self-denial, skips desserts, doesn't eat between meals, and pays little attention to the extravagant things in life, can find such remarkable pleasure and joy with as little as a special flavored tea, or a butterscotch hard candy, a nicely scented lotion, a cool summer breeze, or even the taste of a warm muffin. So many in our society and our culture have been smothered with such decadence that it is almost impossible for them to recognize those things in life that can bring simple pleasure.

One of the greatest powers in life is the use of contrast. Think of a candle that is lit outside during the sunniest part of the day and then contrast that same candle lit in the darkness of a cave. It is the same candle and it is projecting the same amount of light. However, it is in contrast to the environment that it presents so differently. This can be the same in our own lives. By removing all the excess from our lives, living simply, and purging the decadence from our lives, we then become able to see so clearly the contrast of so many things around us. Then when we do experience something outside of our usual exposure, even with the slightest degree of difference, it can be relished so grandly. Truly, less is often more in this life.

EXERCISE – Think of the things in your life that you are becoming to realize might be in excesses and maybe even preventing you from experiencing the simple pleasures available to you. Please list five of them and then consider making a change related to those identified items.

1. _____
2. _____
3. _____
4. _____
5. _____

Let us pray,

Lord, make me an instrument of your peace:
where there is hatred, let me sow love;
where there is injury, pardon;
where there is doubt, faith;
where there is despair, hope;
where there is darkness, light;
where there is sadness, joy.
O divine Master, grant that I may not so much seek
to be consoled as to console,
to be understood as to understand,
to be loved as to love.
For it is in giving that we receive,
it is in pardoning that we are pardoned,
and it is in dying that we are born to eternal life.
Amen.

Day 27

Alcohol and Concupiscence

Alcohol is enjoyed by a large percent of the population in the United States as well as other places around the world. Some even proclaim that it is one of the greatest gifts created by God. Others cite that Jesus' first miracle included turning water into wine so that must be an endorsement for the miraculous drink. Like many things in life, the object itself is not good or bad but rather is dependent on how it is used and utilized. For many, a glass of wine after work, or a few beers on the weekend not only helps with relaxation, but also brings some joy. For others, drinking a fifth a whiskey a day, or downing a twelve-pack after work clearly indicates a disordered use and more than likely is being used as some sort of coping mechanism, albeit ineffectively.

Most of us already know or have experienced the effect that alcohol can have on our inhibitions. After a few drinks, many people find themselves doing things they usually would not have done without the effects of alcohol. Some people find this experience to be rewarding if the action helps them, as an example, it might assist them in overcoming excessive shyness and they become more confident and able to more freely socialize with others. However, some may experience that they do things impulsively when they drink and find that the next day, they have the necessity to deal with some of the negative consequences of their actions. Another aspect related to the use of alcohol has to do with our concupiscence. Remember our concupiscence is the effect of original sin on humanity and explains the cause for why we humans have a tendency toward sin.

For many of us, our conscience and our moral beliefs, as well as our grace-filled willpower are at a constant state of battle against our inner desires to turn away from God and sin. For the most part, as Christians who are trying to live good, honorable, and holy lives, we are able to win that battle a great deal of the time. For some, the trouble comes when we introduce alcohol into the mix of that battle. Alcohol has the unique effect of weakening our defenses when it comes to keeping certain impulses in check, as well as clouding our intellect and preventing us from adequately discerning certain situations that includes anticipating possible consequences from our actions. Now there is a spectrum of these possible consequences as it relates to the use of alcohol and differs with everyone. However, for most, if we are honest, we will not be able to say that excess alcohol makes us a more fervent and holy Christian and strengthens our resolve to fight against temptations and sin. The truth would be that it does quite the opposite.

Regarding the *100 days to Freedom* program, fasting from alcohol during the program is a temporary discipline that allows the participant to be freed from the potential weakening of the resolve to maintain the adherence to the disciplines. Additionally, as we are delving into the spiritual exercises of prayer, meditation, and reflection, we need our heads and minds to be clear to experience the fruits from our efforts and to be able to recognize the changes that are occurring in our lives. The abstinence is also a good discerning tool to see if maybe we have been using alcohol in excess and if it has become an obstacle for spiritual growth in our lives. The abstinence also gives our bodies a time to heal and rejuvenate especially if we have routinely abused the use of alcohol.

Alcohol, as it is present in wine, beer, hard liquor, and other tinctures, is not a bad thing in itself, quite the contrary. Used in moderation it can be a nice addition to our lives to lighten our worries, calm our anxieties, and warm our hearts.

EXERCISE – Think about how you have used alcohol in your life. Is it used in moderation? Has it become a problem for you in the past? Do you feel it has affected your ability to fight against temptation or has it triggered an impulsive response that you would have normally been able to restrain from doing? What does it do for you in a positive manner, if anything? Now being without it for almost a month has anything changed in your life? Do you think you will change how you use and enjoy alcohol in the future?

Let us pray,

Thank You, Lord, for all who have been rescued from alcoholism and for those that have supported them through it. We know that the enemy comes to steal and to kill and to destroy men and women, by enticing them into a life of alcoholism and other evil addictions, but we thank and praise You that Jesus came to destroy the works of the evil one and promised to give life abundantly, to all who trust in Christ as Savior.

Amen.

Day 28

Congratulations, you have made it to day 28. This is a good time to stop, take a deep breath, and to evaluate how well, or maybe how not so well, the disciplines are going. Please take a minute, break out a pen or pencil, and complete this very important self-evaluation regarding adherence.

Spiritual	1 No Action	2 Almost none	3 Hit and miss	4 Almost perfect	5 Nailed it!
Daily Mass or Daily Mass readings and Spiritual Communion					
Daily Rosary					
Formal Examination of Conscience nightly					
Daily Spiritual reading					
Weekly adoration in front of the Blessed Sacrament					
Monthly Confession					

Physical	1 No Action	2 Almost none	3 Hit and miss	4 Almost perfect	5 Nailed it!
Walk or Run daily					
Push-ups / Sit-ups / Lunges daily or weight lifting					
Stretches daily					
7-8 hours' sleep a night					

Nutrition	1 No Action	2 Almost none	3 Hit and miss	4 Almost perfect	5 Nailed it!
2-3 meals a day - No eating between meals					
No candy / desserts					
No fast-food					
Fasting on Mon / Wed / Friday					

Self-Denial	1 No Action	2 Almost none	3 Hit and miss	4 Almost perfect	5 Nailed it!
No major purchases (Toiletries and needed items only)					
No TV or movies					
No social media					
No Alcohol					

Well, how did you do? Let me guess, maybe less than perfect? Join the club, I have yet to meet the perfect human or the one who completed the entire *100 days to Freedom* program without missing a discipline even once. That makes you normal, human, and maybe a little less than a superhero. Yet, as Christians, we are called toward a path of perfection, a life of holiness, a life in which we journey closer and closer to God.

The structure of this program will allow each of us to grow, to grow in virtue, character, self-discipline, and in relationship with God. Reflect once again on the scores you gave yourself above and then on the categories: Spiritual Life, Physical Health, Nutritional Health, and Self-Discipline. If you identify an area where there is more opportunity for growth, then try to place a greater focus on that area for the next week.

We have all been created in God's image and likeness, and we have been created as unique individuals. No two journeys are alike, just like no two scorecards are exactly alike. God is working in us in the exact way He feels that He needs to work in us to help us to travel our unique journey. Let go and allow Him to drive this journey. Our part is to be open to His promptings and respond when He calls.

Keep up the good work and as you progress day-by-day be prepared to enjoy the rewards that God has ready for you. Whenever we turn our focus away from ourselves and upon the Lord, we begin to realize what freedom truly feels and looks like.

Let us pray,

Father, look upon our weakness and reach out to help us with Your loving power.
You redeem us and make us Your children in Christ.
Look upon us, give us true freedom and bring us to the inheritance You promised.
We ask this through our Lord Jesus Christ, Your Son,
who lives and reigns with You and the Holy Spirit,
one God, forever and ever. Amen.

Day 29

Thinking and Behaving

There is an ancient saying in Latin, "Lex orandi, lex credenda," loosely translated, "The law of what is to be prayed [is] the law of what is to be believed." For Christians, this means that prayer and belief are integral to each other and that liturgy is not distinct from theology. It also supports the idea that what we believe is what we pray, and what we pray is what we believe. Our beliefs affect our thinking and our thinking and believing also affect our behavior. What we choose to believe, or have been given the grace of understanding and in turn a belief, directly guides our actions and behaviors. Think about this for a minute. If we believe that killing is wrong, then more than likely we would choose not to kill. If we thought that there was nothing wrong with killing someone, then if the situation presented itself, we would have no hesitation in our action to kill. What about stealing? If one thought it was alright to steal, then they would have no problem taking things from others. What if a person saw all people with equal dignity unrelated to the race, gender, socioeconomic class, or even those who choose to sin? Would that affect how we would act and behave toward various people in life? What if we believed that everyone was basically good, or at least that they would like to be good and that at times they did bad things (Sin)? Would that affect how we choose to see people around us? Would our initial thought about people be positive rather than negative?

Many Scripture verses describe how one might think, believe, and act toward others. Here in the Gospel of Matthew is just one of those examples:

"Stop judging, that you may not be judged. For as you judge, so will you be judged, and the measure with which you measure will be measured out to you. Why do you notice the splinter in your brother's eye, but do not perceive the wooden beam in your own eye? How can you say to your brother, 'Let me remove that splinter from your eye,' while the wooden beam is in your eye? You hypocrite, remove the

wooden beam from your eye first; then you will see clearly to remove the splinter from your brother's eye." (Matthew 7:1-5)

A critical mind might respond to this message with a question such as, "What do you mean that I should never judge? Don't I need to judge if crossing a busy street is dangerous? Or if I should allow my child to visit a friend's home that might not be supervised well?" These are fair questions, and yes there is a degree of discerning and judging that we all must due especially as it relates to being prudent. However, this line of questioning is missing the core of the Scripture message. For many of us, we can become so judgmental of those in our lives that we seldom take a close and revealing look at ourselves. Could it be that the more we keep our judgment focused elsewhere the more likely we will be prevented from seeing our own faults and identifying just how uncharitable we have become?

Returning to the idea that what we believe affects how we think, and how we think affects how we act and behave, maybe we should spend a day thinking about how we can begin to shape our thoughts about others and our world to be more Christ-like. Let's try to listen to how we talk. Pay close attention to the words we choose. Do they reflect our beliefs? Pay attention to your thoughts as you experience different situations in your life. Do these thoughts reflect our Christian beliefs? The more we become cognizant of how we think and speak about things the more we will also become aware of how we are reacting and behaving. As we purposefully choose to change how we think, our actions will automatically change as well. Also, the more our actions change, the more our thinking changes too.

Let us pray,

O Holy Ghost, divine Spirit of light and love, I consecrate to Thee my understanding, my heart and my will, my whole being for time and for eternity.

May my understanding be always obedient to Thy heavenly inspirations and the teachings of the Holy Catholic Church, of which Thou art the infallible Guide;

may my heart be ever inflamed with love of God and of my neighbor;

may my will be ever conformed to the divine will, and may my whole life be a faithful following of the life and virtues of Our Lord and Savior Jesus Christ, to whom with the Father and Thee be honor and glory forever.
Amen.

Day 30

Thankfulness

Has our society and culture become thankless? Have I become an unthankful person? Have I developed an entitled attitude in what I expect, or at least have become accustomed to having things the way I want them and when I want them? Have I become so desensitized by the reception of so many gifts that when I do receive them, they go without mentioning? In the Gospel of Luke, there is a message for us to ponder as we travel through our *100 days to Freedom* journey.

As Jesus continued his journey to Jerusalem, he traveled through Samaria and Galilee.
As he was entering a village, ten lepers met him.
They stood at a distance from him and raised their voices, saying, "Jesus, Master! Have pity on us!"
And when he saw them, he said, "Go show yourselves to the priests."
As they were going they were cleansed.
And one of them, realizing he had been healed, returned, glorifying God in a loud voice;
and he fell at the feet of Jesus and thanked him.
He was a Samaritan.
Jesus said in reply, "Ten were cleansed, were they not?
Where are the other nine?
Has none but this foreigner returned to give thanks to God?"
Then he said to him, "Stand up and go; your faith has saved you." (Luke 17:11-19)

All ten of the lepers had been healed from their disease, but only one returned to give thanks. And of the ten, it wasn't even one of the Jews who returned, but an outsider to the faith, a Samaritan. This Gospel message should give us all pause to think about our relationship with God. When we ask favors or His help with intervention, and when we receive a response are we quick to give thanks? Are aware that

God often knows our needs even before we do, and that He places people and events in our lives to help us in the areas that we need help? Knowing this, when good things happen in our lives are we quick to respond to God and give our thankfulness to Him, to the one who either wills or allows everything wonderful in this world to occur?

EXERCISE – List five positive things that have occurred in your life over the past few years.

1. _____
2. _____
3. _____
4. _____
5. _____

Who do you think was behind those positive things gifted to you? Did you thank all involved with those events, not only God which should be expected but everyone else that participated in those occurrences?

Finding true happiness in life includes being able to see all the wonderful things that are occurring around us each day and possessing a humble heart, not expecting those things to occur, but being cognizant when they do happen and then immediately showing our gratitude for all involved especially our Creator, Savior, and Lord.

Let us pray,

Father in Heaven, Creator of all, and source of all goodness and love,
please look kindly upon us and receive our heartfelt gratitude in this time of giving thanks.
Thank you for all the graces and blessings You have bestowed upon us, spiritual and temporal:
our faith and religious heritage, our food and shelter, our health, the love we have for one another,
our family and friends.
Dear Father, in Your infinite generosity, please grant us continued graces
and blessings throughout the coming year.
We ask this through our Lord Jesus Christ, your Son,
who lives and reigns with you and the Holy Spirit, one God, forever and ever. Amen.

Day 31

Life Balance

Over the years we have all heard the saying that we need to keep our lives balanced. Have you ever stopped to think about what that really means, especially how that translates to your life? When we think of balance most people think of things like work, family, friends, hobbies, etc. Others when they hear the word balance, immediately think of rest, desiring to have more rest and less work. Let's take a moment and think about God and what He did as written in the book of Genesis. He took (worked) 6 days to create the world, man and woman, animals, oceans, and the sky, and on the 7th day, He rested. I know these days do not represent literal days as we know them, but let's focus on the proportionality. It wasn't a 50/50 mix. He didn't work for 3 ½ days and then took 3 ½ days off to rest. God taught that balanced, especially regarding work and rest, doesn't necessarily need to equal. Now let's think about our own work week, most of us work 5-6 days a week and rest 1-2 days a week. Looks a lot like the example God modeled for us doesn't it? Maybe a better explanation of balance would mean having everything in its proper place and portioned appropriately.

Making decisions about creating balance in one's life also takes discernment. There is only so much time in the day and that time needs to be divided between our responsibilities and our desires. One that has a family will need to take into consideration how many hours each day they work to provide for the family while at the same time deciding how much time they will choose to be at home and physically present and available to the family. One needs to carefully identify what their priorities are in life and let that decision help with making future choices. If a person decides to work extra to help build monetary treasure, it is often at the cost of spending less time with the family. If one chooses to spend a great deal of time with the family, then they have less available time to dedicate to earning money. The same is true for charity work, serving at church, serving the poor, and coaching or mentoring others. For every "Yes" we give to an opportunity, we are also saying "No" to something else in our lives. Again, no one can do it all, there is just so many hours in a day, and so much energy we have to offer. We must prioritize what is important in our lives and use that knowledge and understanding as our guide for achieving a balanced life.

EXERCISE – Please list what are the most important things in your life. What are your priorities?

1. _____
2. _____
3. _____
4. _____
5. _____

What are some of the things you might need to say "No" to, to maintain your priorities?

1. _____
2. _____
3. _____
4. _____
5. _____

Let us pray,

Lord, help me to create a balanced life.
Help me to take time to enjoy life, to be a person full of gratitude.
Help me take time to love, to extend my hand in service to those around me.
Lord, remind me to take time to learn, to be disciplined and accountable.
Help me to make a difference in the small and big moments of my life.
Lord, help me to keep smiling, to be happy, and to try to be myself.
Lord, infuse me with Your Spirit so I can create a life of balance, moderation, and simplicity.
And whatever my challenge, let it be an occasion to deepen my life's purpose.
Amen.

Day 32

Knowing Our Path

So many people struggle in life trying to identify what their path in life should be. They read books, they go to seminars, and some even seek out gurus of various types to help them to see what they are unable to see themselves. Yet, it really is much simpler than one might think. God has the tendency to lead us toward the type of life he had envisioned for us, created us for, and desired us to complete. He often uses not only our successes but even our failures in life to progressively guide us. We only need to be aware of how He is working in our lives to see how He is forming us. The first step in identifying our path is to discern what type of person God desires for us to be. This can be done by a focused reflection on the events of our lives in the light of virtues. As we begin to identify the joyful, glorious, and even the sorrowful events in our lives we can begin to see some common themes. One example would be to look at the sorrowful events of our lives and then consider how God might be using those situations to develop or deepen a certain virtue such as forgiveness, patience, or love. We can then reflect on the joyful and glorious events of our lives while also identifying what God was trying to reinforce in our lives through those experiences. An example: the virtues found in marriage might reflect commitment, service, or selfless love. The more events we evaluate and reflect upon, the more we can begin to see common themes emerging or patterns revealed. This exercise is best done after going to confession and removing any sinfulness from our soul and allowing God's grace the full access to our intellect. Then we can ask in prayer for God to reveal the events and situations that might have gone unnoticed for some time. Taking a pen, we can then begin to write done the events that pop into our minds. Once we have an extensive list of memorable events, we can then identify what is the prominent virtue in each experience. Once each memory has been given a corresponding virtue we can then gather and group those virtues together into 2, 3, or 4 groups. Once you have done so, then even more clearly you will begin to see a pattern. This pattern is a revelation of how God has been working in your life over the years, usually unnoticed, and to develop certain virtues or traits in you, for you to grow into the version of the person God had always wanted you to become. Those gathered memories and corresponding virtues might look something like this: Humble, Loving, and Faithful. So, what does this mean? It means that God has been helping you, either directly, or as a result of your free-will actions, to have opportunities in your life to become a more humble, loving, and faithful person. Now, this is just one example. You might find that your list of memories and associated virtues might be more like Forgiving, Persevering, and Loving. Or even: Courageous, Honorable, and Truthful. Whatever the virtues are, it is a clear guide to identifying your path in life. If you have been called to be and are being progressively being formed to become a person that is humble, loving, and kind, then your actions and direction in life should be centered on being just those things. When you make decisions or find yourself in certain situations, you can remind yourself that God has created you to be a humble, loving, and kind person, and that is exactly how you should proceed.

EXERCISE: What are some of your memories in life? This is just a brief example of what an extensive and comprehensive life reviewed would look like, scaled-down. However, by completing this mini-exercise you will understand the process.

Glorious	Memory →			
	Virtue →			
Joyful	Memory →			
	Virtue →			
Sorrowful	Memory →			
	Virtue →			

Let us pray,

Show me Your ways, LORD, teach me Your paths.
Guide me in Your truth and teach me, for You are God my Savior,
and my hope is in You all day long.
Amen. Psalm 25:4-5

Day 33

Creativity

Creativity in one's life is so important for a variety of reasons. It allows an opportunity to express our feelings, frustrations, joys, sorrows, ideas, and even our dreams. Some with musical abilities might choose the piano, guitar, ukulele, or even a kazoo as their mode of expression. Others like to create by drawing and painting. Some have a dramatic flair and pursue the role of a thespian. There are also those who use the written word as a mechanism to explore their imaginary journeys and adventures.

Whatever the mode of expression may be, accessing and utilizing the creative portion of our brain improves our ability to connect the different hemispheres of our most important neurological organ, but is also a catalyst for stimulating thoughts and ideas. The more we desire to be creative, especially when acted upon, the more creative we become. Often in our efforts to be creative: singing, painting, writing, acting, building, drawing, etc., we transcend the perceived restrictions and restraints of our lives and can see and experience many things much differently than we would have without the effort of trying to look outside of the box of routine and normality. Being creative breaks through the mundane in our lives and sparks life in our souls. Yes, these expressions can at times be grandiose, crazy, a little weird, bizarre, silly, and maybe not even relatable to anyone else, but in the effort of the participant, they can be exhilarating and sensational.

Take a moment and think about how you allow yourself to be creative. How do you express yourself? Do you have a hobby that helps you be creative? Is there something you can remember doing that brought you joy but have not done it for some time? Is there a hobby that you have always wanted to start but have never followed through?

EXERCISE – List five things that you do, have done, or thing you might want to try that would allow you to be creative.

1. _____

2. _____

3. _____

4. _____

5. _____

Now the next question is, "What is stopping you from starting this hobby?"

Let us pray,

Dear Lord,

Thank You for all the creation You have brought to life.

Thank You for the incredible gifts and talents that You have so generously entrusted to me.

With Your grace may I appreciate and develop these talents further,

and always recognize that they originated from You and remain Yours.

Please guide me in the use of these gifts so that they will be used well and also for the benefit of others,

and may inspire others to become aware of Your creative presence in their lives.

Help me also to use Your talents, entrusted to me,

to bring a creative spark and new possibilities to Your world,

living out my unique call to be an instrument of Your creative love.

Amen.

Use this section below to journal any thoughts or inspirations from the meditation to help with further reflection.

_____

_____

_____

_____

_____

_____

Day 34

Lust and Impurity

This topic can be quite sensitive and often not spoken of due to various reasons. However, lust, masturbation, and impurity are conditions and acts that wound the soul severely. Lust is defined as a disordered desire for, or an inordinate enjoyment of sexual pleasure especially when sought for itself. Masturbation is sinful because it misuses the gift of sexuality in an inherently selfish act, devoid of love. Impurity speaks to anything that ruins the uncontaminated nature of something.

God created man and woman to be united and to be procreative. This love that is reciprocal is not based solely on the reception of love, although that is an aspect, it is most evident in the selfless giving of love. The unitive aspect of marriage involves the full personhood of the spouses, a love that encompasses the minds, hearts, emotions, bodies, souls, and aspirations of husbands and wives. They are called to grow continually in intimate love and fidelity so that they are no longer two but one flesh. Their mutual self-giving is strengthened and blessed by Jesus Christ in the Sacrament of Matrimony.

Any act of sex outside of marriage is not in line with God's plan and further separates the person from God. We are called to be chaste. Chastity means the successful integration of sexuality within the person and thus the inner unity of man in his bodily and spiritual being. People should cultivate [chastity] in the way that is suited to their state of life. Some profess virginity or consecrated celibacy which enables them to give themselves to God alone with an undivided heart in a remarkable manner. Others live in the way prescribed for all by the moral law, whether they are married or single. Married people are called to live conjugal chastity; others practice chastity in continence. (Catechism of the Catholic Church, #2349)

Those who are engaged to marry are called to live in continence. They should see in this time of testing a discovery of mutual respect, an apprenticeship in fidelity, and hope of receiving one another from

God. They should reserve for marriage the expressions of affection that belong to married love. They will help each other grow in chastity. (Catechism of the Catholic Church, #2350)

Chastity is the joyous affirmation of someone who knows how to live self-giving, free from any form of self-centered slavery. The chaste person is not self-centered, not involved in selfish relationships with other people. Chastity makes the personality harmonious. It matures it and fills it with inner peace. (PCF, The Truth and Meaning of Human Sexuality: Guidelines for Education Within the Family, December 8, 1995, #17)

The more the faithful appreciate the value of chastity and its necessary role in their lives as men and women, the better they will understand, by a kind of spiritual instinct, its moral requirements and counsels. In the same way, they will know better how to accept and carry out, in a spirit of docility to the Church's teaching, what an upright conscience dictates in concrete cases. (CDF, Persona humana, December 29, 1975, XI)

The faithful of the present time, and indeed today more than ever, must use the means which have always been recommended by the Church for living a chaste life. These means are: discipline of the senses and the mind, watchfulness and prudence in avoiding occasions of sin, the observance of modesty, moderation in recreation, wholesome pursuits, assiduous prayer and frequent reception of the Sacraments of Penance and the Eucharist. Young people especially should earnestly foster devotion to the Immaculate Mother of God, and take as examples the lives of saints and other faithful people, especially young ones, who excelled in the practice of chastity. (CDF, Persona humana, December 29, 1975, XII)

Let us pray,

"Dearest Jesus!
I know well that every perfect gift, and above all others that of chastity, depends upon the most powerful assistance of Your Providence, and that without You a creature can do nothing. Therefore, I pray You to defend, with Your grace, chastity, and purity in my soul as well as in my body. And if I have ever received through my senses any impression that could stain my chastity and purity, may You, Who are the Supreme Lord of all my powers, take it from me, that I may with an immaculate heart advance in Your love and service, offering myself chaste all the days of my life on the most pure altar of Your Divinity. Amen."

Day 35

Living the Beatitudes

The Sermon on the Mount.

When He saw the crowds, He went up the mountain, and after He had sat down, His disciples came to Him. He began to teach them, saying:

"Blessed are the poor in spirit, for theirs is the kingdom of heaven.

Blessed are they who mourn, for they will be comforted.

Blessed are the meek, for they will inherit the land.

Blessed are they who hunger and thirst for righteousness, for they will be satisfied.

Blessed are the merciful, for they will be shown mercy.

Blessed are the clean of heart, for they will see God.

Blessed are the peacemakers, for they will be called children of God.

Blessed are they who are persecuted for the sake of righteousness,
for theirs is the kingdom of heaven.

Blessed are you when they insult you and persecute you and utter every kind of evil against you [falsely] because of me.

Rejoice and be glad, for your reward will be great in heaven.

Thus, they persecuted the prophets who were before you."

The Beatitudes are the teachings of Jesus in the Sermon on the Mount (Matthew 5:1-12). Jesus teaches us that if we live according to the Beatitudes, we will live a happy Christian life. The Beatitudes fulfill God's promises made to Abraham and his descendants and describe the rewards that will be ours as loyal followers of Christ.

So many of us are looking for happiness, regrettably, often in all the wrong places. The *100 days to Freedom* program is helping you to simplify your life, your routines, removing unhealthy distractions, and slowly bringing you to a place where you can see things for what they truly are. In a way, this is a journey where through discipline, desire, devotion, dedication, and drive you are slowly being drawn closer to the Divine. You are beginning to see things as God and Christ has desired you to see them, as they truly are, as you truly are. Yes, this truth at times can be difficult, especially when it is revealed that our faults and inadequacies are even greater than we had imagined, Yet, it is in this revelation that we can begin the process of transformation.

The beatitudes are a good place to focus our thoughts today and will help us to grow in virtue.

CHALLENGE – Carry this book with you today, or at least a copy of the beatitudes, and reread the beatitudes at least five times throughout this day. Each time you read them take one of the beatitudes that stands out to you at the time and meditate upon it while looking for a deeper meaning. Begin this reelection by first praying the following prayer and invoking the assistance of the Holy Spirit in this process:

Dear Holy Spirit,
<u>Spirit of wisdom and understanding</u>, enlighten my mind to perceive the
mysteries of the universe in relation to eternity.
<u>Spirit of right judgment and courage</u> guide me and make me firm in
my baptismal decision to follow Jesus' way of love.
<u>Spirit of knowledge and reverence</u> help me to see the lasting value
of justice and mercy in my everyday dealings with others.
<u>Spirit of love</u> help me to meditate on these beatitudes and reveal
their deeper meaning as they relate uniquely to me and my life.
<u>Spirit of God</u> spark my faith, hope, and love into new action each day and
fill my life with wonder and awe in Your presence which penetrates all creation.
Amen.

Day 36

Self-talk can be a powerful influencer in our lives either in a positive or negative way. The way we think and speak, even internally, about ourselves quickly becomes a reflection of who we think we are even if it isn't realistic. In a positive sense, if we think well of ourselves this usually translates into self-confidence and social ease since we project these feelings onto those around us. For the opposite, if we think poorly of ourselves, we most likely also feel that others think of us in a similar way and this tends to promote isolation and withdrawal from others. These negative thoughts do not usually come from God, or Christ, or the Holy Spirit. They are a result of the efforts that come from the devil and his dominions and in some cases might come from our guilt from acting contrary to the way we know we should act and behave. In the case of guilt, these negative feelings might be helpful if we use them as catalysts for making a change. This is most often accomplished by running to the Sacrament of Reconciliation (Confession) and removing the stain of sin from our souls and then vowing to not repeat the behaviors.

As for self-talk in the general sense, and especially when it has to do with negative self-talk, this can become habitual and as mentioned earlier can be quite damaging to the psyche of the person. This is especially true when the negative perception is not based in reality and is not grounded in truth. The best way to overcome this destructive phenomenon is to purposely and with intention begin to think of yourself the way God thinks of you. Stop comparing yourself to others and start to think of your individuality, especially regarding the extreme uniqueness in which you have been created. There is no one else in this entire world with your exact DNA. The is no one else in the entire world with the same brain, soul, and personality. God intentionally made each of us unique and gave us talents and gifts that are individualistically yours. He also gave you certain weaknesses knowing that they would become your cross and that you would struggle with them while developing enhanced virtues and deepening your character and resolve as you learn to not only deal with these weaknesses but find ways to minimize their effects. These weaknesses are also used to keep us humble and also to ever so often remind us of our need to rely on God and not ourselves since we truly are powerless without God.

EXERCISE – take a moment and list some of the negative self-talk phrases you find filling your mind from time to time and then make a list of how you perceive God in His Divine Mercy and Love looks at you.

Negative Self-Talk Examples

1. _____
2. _____
3. _____
4. _____
5. _____

How God looks at you as His Loving Creation

1. _____
2. _____
3. _____
4. _____
5. _____

Make it a practice beginning today that every time you find that negative self-talk has begun to fill your mind, you replace those thoughts with the positive thoughts of how God sees you as His Loving Creation. This simple exercise has a powerful effect of one's mood, perception of the world around them, how they relate to others, and overtime can even change the chemistry of the brain in such a way that there are lasting and irrevocable positive effects.

Let us pray,

Dear loving Father,
shield me so that the enemy has no way to enter in.
I humbly request the Holy Spirit's presence be thrusted upon my life,
as He guides my thoughts in the direction of positivity.
Change my thought patterns, Oh Lord my God, to be focused on You and Your promises.
Dear Lord, I pray that today, You give me the strength to control my thoughts.
Lead me in a plain path and fill my soul with Your grace. Amen.

Day 37

The Ten Commandments

According to Exodus in the Old Testament, God issued his own set of laws (the Ten Commandments) to Moses on Mount Sinai. In Catholicism, the Ten Commandments are considered divine law because God himself revealed them and because they were spelled out specifically with no room for ambiguity. The Ten Commandments are a description of the basic freedom from sin that is necessary to live as a Christian. They are <u>a minimum level of living</u>, below which we must not go. The Ten Commandments and Catholicism have been bound together since the time of Christ. In fact, Jesus refers to the Ten Commandments and assures their validity in his dialog with the rich young man in Matthew's Gospel (Mt 19:16-21).

It's important to note that each Commandment is simply a summary of a whole category of actions. Don't be legalistic, searching for a way around them because their wording doesn't fit you perfectly! For example, "bearing false witness against your neighbor" covers any kind of falsehood: perjury, lying, slander, detraction, rash judgment, etc.

The Catholic Ten Commandments are linked together to form a coherent whole. If you break one of them, you're guilty of breaking all of them (Catechism of the Catholic Church, #2069). The Commandments express man's fundamental duties to God and neighbor. As such, they represent grave obligations. To violate them knowingly & willingly in a significant way is to commit a mortal sin.

The Catholic tradition uses the division of the Commandments established by St. Augustine. Here are the Catholic Ten Commandments:

1. I am the LORD your God. You shall worship the Lord your God and Him only shall you serve.
2. You shall not take the name of the Lord your God in vain.
3. Remember to keep holy the Sabbath day.
4. Honor your father and your mother.
5. You shall not kill.
6. You shall not commit adultery.
7. You shall not steal.
8. You shall not bear false witness against your neighbor.
9. You shall not covet your neighbor's wife.
10. You shall not covet your neighbor's goods.

EXERCISE – Take a few minutes and reread the Commandments and then reflect upon them as they relate to your life. It is honorable to memorize them. Practice memorizing them today. You will be surprised at how quickly they can be learned and retained. As the *100 days to Freedom* journey continues, we will periodically explore each Commandment one by one in more depth.

Let us pray,

Heavenly Father,
Open my heart, my mind, and my soul
to abide joyfully in your guidance through the Commandments
so that I may live a life of freedom and joy.
Amen.

Use this section below to journal any thoughts or inspirations from the meditation to help with further reflection.

_____
_____
_____
_____
_____
_____

Day 38

The Devil

Behind the disobedient choice of our first parents lurks a seductive voice, opposed to God, which makes them fall into death out of envy. Scripture and the Church's Tradition sees in this being a fallen angel, called "Satan" or the "devil". The Church teaches that Satan was at first a good angel, made by God: "The devil and the other demons were indeed created naturally good by God, but they became evil by their own doing."

Scripture speaks of the sin of these angels. This "fall" consists in the free choice of these created spirits, who radically and irrevocably rejected God and his reign. We find a reflection of that rebellion in the tempter's words to our first parents: "You will be like God." The devil "has sinned from the beginning"; he is "a liar and the father of lies".

It is the irrevocable character of their choice, and not a defect in the infinite divine mercy, that makes the angels' sin unforgivable. "There is no repentance for the angels after their fall, just as there is no repentance for men after death."

Scripture witnesses to the disastrous influence of the one Jesus calls "a murderer from the beginning", who would even try to divert Jesus from the mission received from his Father, "The reason the Son of God appeared was to destroy the works of the devil." In its consequences, the gravest of these works was the mendacious seduction that led man to disobey God.

The power of Satan is, nonetheless, not infinite. He is only a creature, powerful from the fact that he is pure spirit, but still a creature. He cannot prevent the building up of God's reign. Although Satan may act in the world out of hatred for God and his kingdom in Christ Jesus, and although his action may cause grave injuries - of a spiritual nature and, indirectly, even of a physical nature - to each man and to society, the action is permitted by divine providence which with strength and gentleness guides human and cosmic history. It is a great mystery that providence should permit diabolical activity, but "we know that in everything God works for good with those who love him."

Take note of Pope Francis' words about the devil, "We should not think of the devil as a myth, a representation, a symbol, a figure of speech or an idea. This mistake would leave us to let down our guard, to grow careless and end up more vulnerable. Taking advantage of that vulnerability, the devil does not need to possess us. He poisons us with the venom of hatred, desolation, envy, and vice."

CHALLENGE – Take a few moments and think about how the devil may be working in your life trying to separate you from the ways of the Lord and the life of a Christian.

Let us pray,

Immaculate Heart!
Help us to conquer the menace of evil,
which so easily takes root in the hearts of the people of today,
and whose immeasurable effects already weigh down upon
our modern world and seem to block the paths towards the future!
From famine and war, deliver us.
From nuclear war, from incalculable self-destruction, from every kind of war, deliver us.
From sins against the life of man from its very beginning, deliver us.
From hatred and from the demeaning of the dignity of the children of God, deliver us.
From every kind of injustice in the life of society, both national and international, deliver us.
From readiness to trample on the commandments of God, deliver us.
From attempts to stifle in human hearts the very truth of God, deliver us.
From the loss of awareness of good and evil, deliver us.
From sins against the Holy Spirit, deliver us, deliver us.
Accept, O Mother of Christ, this cry laden with the sufferings of
all individual human beings, laden with the sufferings of whole societies.
Help us with the power of the Holy Spirit to conquer all sin: individual sin
and the "sin of the world", sin in all its manifestations.
Let there be revealed, once more, in the history of the world
the infinite saving power of the Redemption: the power of merciful Love!
May it put a stop to evil! May it transform consciences!
May your Immaculate Heart reveal for all the light of Hope!
Amen.

-Saint John Paul II, Consecration of all Individuals and Peoples of the World to the Immaculate Heart of Mary, 1984

Day 39

Humility

Of all the sins in the world, PRIDE is the one most prevalent. Often, we are not even aware of how much we are affected by our pride. The opposite of pride is humility and we should purposefully seek to become humbler every day.

How do we gain the mind of Christ and humble ourselves? To put on the mind of Christ, we will need to make a firm decision to ponder, understand, and adopt Jesus' way of thinking; his values and attitudes must become ours. His strong emphasis on humility and meekness and his example of it must take hold of our thinking, our desires, and our conduct. We must admire his humility and want it for ourselves. For this to happen, we need to earnestly and regularly pray for the Holy Spirit to change our hearts, for it is impossible to do it in our own strength. We will also need to understand what Jesus meant when he called men and women to humble themselves.

We discover that from the Greek word Jesus and the apostles used, tapeinos, which conveys the idea of having a right view of ourselves before God and others. If pride is an exalted sense of who we are in relation to God and others, humility is having a realistic sense of who we are before God and others. We must not think too highly (or too lowly) of ourselves. Rather, we must be honest and realistic about who and what we are.

EXERCISE – Think on someone in your life, present or past, who you would consider being a very humble person. List three attributes of that person that you feel were at the core of their humility.

1. _____
2. _____
3. _____

Let us pray,

Litany of Humility

O Jesus! meek and humble of heart, Hear me.

From the desire of being esteemed,

Deliver me, Jesus.

From the desire of being loved...

From the desire of being extolled ...

From the desire of being honored ...

From the desire of being praised ...

From the desire of being preferred to others...

From the desire of being consulted ...

From the desire of being approved ...

From the fear of being humiliated ...

From the fear of being despised...

From the fear of suffering rebukes ...

From the fear of being calumniated ...

From the fear of being forgotten ...

From the fear of being ridiculed ...

From the fear of being wronged ...

From the fear of being suspected ...

That others may be loved more than I,

Jesus, grant me the grace to desire it.

That others may be esteemed more than I ...

That, in the opinion of the world,

others may increase and I may decrease ...

That others may be chosen and I set aside ...

That others may be praised and I unnoticed ...

That others may be preferred to me in everything...

That others may become holier than I, provided that I may become as holy as I should...

Amen.

Day 40

The First Commandment

I am the LORD your God. You shall worship the Lord your God and Him only shall you serve.

God makes himself known by recalling his all-powerful loving, and liberating action in the history of the one he addresses: "I brought you out of the land of Egypt, out of the house of bondage." The first word contains the First Commandment of the Law: "You shall fear the LORD your God; you shall serve him. . . . You shall not go after other gods." God's first call and just demand is that man accept him and worship him.

The First Commandment embraces faith, hope, and charity. When we say 'God' we confess a constant, unchangeable being, always the same, faithful and just, without any evil. It follows that we must necessarily accept his words and have complete faith in him and acknowledge his authority. He is almighty, merciful, and infinitely beneficent. Who could not place all hope in him? Who could not love him when contemplating the treasures of goodness and love he has poured out on us? Hence the formula God employs in the Scripture at the beginning and end of his commandments: 'I am the LORD.'

Faith - Our moral life has its source in faith in God who reveals his love to us. St. Paul speaks of the "obedience of faith" as our first obligation. He shows that "ignorance of God" is the principle and explanation of all moral deviations. Our duty toward God is to believe in him and to bear witness to him.

Hope - When God reveals Himself and calls him, man cannot fully respond to the divine love by his own powers. He must hope that God will give him the capacity to love Him in return and to act in conformity with the commandments of charity. Hope is the confident expectation of divine blessing and the beatific vision of God; it is also the fear of offending God's love and of incurring punishment.

Charity - Faith in God's love encompasses the call and the obligation to respond with sincere love to divine charity. The First Commandment enjoins us to love God above everything and all creatures for him and because of him.

One can sin against God's love in various ways:

- indifference neglects or refuses to reflect on divine charity; it fails to consider its prevenient goodness and denies its power.
- ingratitude fails or refuses to acknowledge divine charity and to return Him love for love.
- lukewarmness is hesitation or negligence in responding to divine love; it can imply refusal to give oneself over to the prompting of charity.
- acedia or spiritual sloth goes so far as to refuse the joy that comes from God and to be repelled by divine goodness.
- hatred of God comes from pride. It is contrary to the love of God, whose goodness it denies, and whom it presumes to curse as the one who forbids sins and inflicts punishments.

EXERCISE – Reflect on these last five bullet points especially in relation to your life. Ask yourself this question: "Have I been indifferent, ungrateful, lukewarm in my faith, spiritually sloth, and shown pride?

Let us pray,

God, my Father,
may I love You in all things and above all things.
May I reach the joy which You have prepared for me in Heaven.
Nothing is good that is against Your Will,
and all that is good comes from Your Hand.
Place in my heart a desire to please You
and fill my mind with thoughts of Your Love,
so that I may grow in Your Wisdom and enjoy Your Peace.
Amen.

Day 41

Core Concepts

Let us take a few moments and reflect upon some of the core concepts/situations that brought many to the *100 days to Freedom* program and fueled their desire for transformation. The following bullet points reflect the "why" for so many.

- They had developed sinful habits and used vice (alcohol, overeating, gambling, pornography, movie, TV, internet (social media) binging, excessive shopping and spending, drugs, etc.) to compensate for, or numb a deeper problem, and they had become dependent on them.
- They had lost, or maybe never had developed appropriate discipline in their lives.
- The concept of self-denial had become foreign to them.
- Sacrifice only occurred when forced upon them and self-sacrifice was non-present in their lives.
- Even though many of them claimed to be Catholic or Christian, much in their lives would not support that and they were truly lukewarm at best in fervency.
- They were not as virtuous as they should have been.
- Deep down they knew that God had created them to be more than what they were presenting, but they did not know how to change that.
- Their prayer life was almost non-existent, or they had lost the ability to feel fulfilled in prayer.
- Their relationship with God, Jesus, and the Holy Spirit seemed distant and far from intimate.
- They had no idea of what a holy habit was, at least not in their lives.

The above list is enough to make almost anyone depressed, especially if they could check off more than a few of those bullet points as true in their own lives. What about you, how many of those bullet points reflected you at the start of this journey. Yet, does that really matter now? You probably are already feeling that some of those bullet points listed above have become less and less true in your life. You have regained hope and inspiration by the changes you have already seen.

The journey is not even half over yet, and what has been covered is just the beginning, the foundation. With each additional week the graces, the change, and the transformation will begin to intensify and exponentially multiply in power and force. Fasten your seat belts, keep focused, dig in and increase your compliance to the disciplines, and get ready to see just how positive and sensational the additional growth and transformation will be.

Congratulations on responding to God's grace and accepting the challenge, the *100 days to Freedom* program, and for saying "Yes" to the Holy Spirit encouraging you to transform your life. You have already begun, 41 days ago, a journey that will forever change your life.

Let us pray,

Dear Lord, I pray that I do not become like the world. I pray that I am transformed by the renewing of my mind that I may learn to understand Your will for my life, which is good and pleasing and perfect. I thank You for my spiritual growth and transformation, help me focus on the godly values and ethical attitudes that will help me flourish spiritually, emotionally and mentally, Amen.

Use this section below to journal any thoughts or inspirations from the meditation to help with further reflection.

Day 42

Congratulations, you have made it to day 42 (6 weeks). This is a good time to stop, take a deep breath, and to evaluate how well, or maybe how not so well, the disciplines are going. Please take a minute, break out a pen or pencil, and complete this very important self-evaluation regarding adherence.

Spiritual	1 No Action	2 Almost none	3 Hit and miss	4 Almost perfect	5 Nailed it!
Daily Mass or Daily Mass readings and Spiritual Communion					
Daily Rosary					
Formal Examination of Conscience nightly					
Daily Spiritual reading					
Weekly adoration in front of the Blessed Sacrament					
Monthly Confession					

Physical	1 No Action	2 Almost none	3 Hit and miss	4 Almost perfect	5 Nailed it!
Walk or Run daily					
Push-ups / Sit-ups / Lunges daily or weight lifting					
Stretches daily					
7-8 hours' sleep a night					

Nutrition	1 No Action	2 Almost none	3 Hit and miss	4 Almost perfect	5 Nailed it!
2-3 meals a day - No eating between meals					
No candy / desserts					
No fast-food					
Fasting on Mon / Wed / Friday					

Self-Denial	1 No Action	2 Almost none	3 Hit and miss	4 Almost perfect	5 Nailed it!
No major purchases (Toiletries and needed items only)					
No TV or movies					
No social media					
No Alcohol					

Well, how did you do? Let me guess, maybe less than perfect? Join the club, I have yet to meet the perfect human or the one who completed the entire *100 days to Freedom* program without missing a discipline even once. That makes you normal, human, and maybe a little less than a superhero. Yet, as Christians, we are called toward a path of perfection, a life of holiness, a life in which we journey closer and closer to God.

The structure of this program will allow each of us to grow, to grow in virtue, character, self-discipline, and in relationship with God. Reflect once again on the scores you gave yourself above and then on the categories: Spiritual Life, Physical Health, Nutritional Health, and Self-Discipline. If you identify an area where there is more opportunity for growth, then try to place a greater focus on that area for the next week.

We have all been created in God's image and likeness, and we have been created as unique individuals. No two journeys are alike, just like no two scorecards are exactly alike. God is working in us in the exact way He feels that He needs to work in us to help us to travel our unique journey. Let go and allow Him to drive this journey. Our part is to be open to His promptings and respond when He calls.

Keep up the good work and as you progress day-by-day be prepared to enjoy the rewards that God has ready for you. Whenever we turn our focus away from ourselves and upon the Lord, we begin to realize what freedom truly feels and looks like.

Let us pray,

Father, look upon our weakness and reach out to help us with Your loving power.
You redeem us and make us Your children in Christ.
Look upon us, give us true freedom and bring us to the inheritance You promised.
We ask this through our Lord Jesus Christ, Your Son,
who lives and reigns with You and the Holy Spirit,
one God, forever and ever. Amen.

Day 43

Fear of Death – Faith brings Hope

How often in our lives to do we talk about our death and the end of life with those around us, especially those close to us like our spouses, family, and friends? It is much easier to talk about the death of others than it is to talk about our own death.

As Catholics, we are to be living our lives in preparation for death. A life well-lived, especially regarding a life well-lived in the faith, brings about a comfortable death and ease of transition from this life to the next. But why is it that so many of us fear death? Fear of death comes from a lack of faith and hope. Faith is the foundation of our spiritual life that we are to have as Catholics, and it is with this faith that brings us hope. It is that hope that brings us courage in the light of difficulty, even when that difficulty includes the possibility of death. That hope is the understanding that there will be life after death, a life of such love, peace, and tranquility like we have never seen or experienced before.

So how does this all come about? Like many things in life, it begins in the family. The Father brings faith and truth into the home. Not exclusively, but that is his role and task. The wife embraces that faith and truth, internalizes it, and turns it into love and charity. It is the wife who is the heart and love of the home. And when the father who is faith, mixes with the wife who is love, working together, springs forth hope. With faith and hope, we are able to combat fear. The fear of death is only present when we are lacking faith and hope in our lives. Especially because it is faith and hope that specifically brings forth courage.

Don't we all want the grace of a happy death? At this point, you might be asking how is it that we can embrace our Catholic lives, our Catholic faith, be living our lives well, and how to be prepared for when difficult times come, especially times that might involve death. First of all, we are to do the basics of what it means to be Catholic.

- We are to speak and listen to God daily in prayer.
- We are to attend weekly Mass and Holy Days of Obligation.
- We should cleanse our souls quickly every time it becomes stained with mortal sin.
- We are to be charitable with our time, talents, and treasure.
- We are to learn our faith and especially what the church teaches about death so that we are well prepared to make the right decisions for ourselves and for our loved ones.

If we are desiring to have a peaceful and comfortable death, we need to live our lives well, and to make sure we share our thoughts and ideas about death with those the closest to us. Because the time may come when we are not able to communicate our desires and we will be relying on others to make those decisions for us. These decisions often include such things as being placed on a ventilator, having feeding tubes placed or not placed, performing or not performing CPR, just to mention a few. Can you imagine the stress placed on an individual who must make these decisions for someone else when they truly do not know what the person would have desired? There are many mechanisms available for a person to document their specific desires to be honored for such a time, like Advance Directives, Living Wills, and Durable Powers of Attorney for Health Care. These documents are easily available and can be obtained often for free on the internet and from physician's offices, but they do not take the place of sitting down with one's family and discussing how exactly one feels about death and the processes surrounding it.

There are many practical things that can be done and should be done, well in advance, as previously mentioned, to clearly give guidance to family, friends, and care providers, describing what your wishes are regarding what to do and not to do if a time comes where you cannot speak for yourself. This will ensure your wishes are honored and will prevent any unnecessary stress on others. We should also ensure that we clearly understand the teachings of our faith on end of life issues by speaking to an informed priest, deacon, or others knowledgeable in the faith. One can also reference the Catechism of the Catholic Church for sound advice. Additionally, we should be focused on living a life "well-lived" in the faith. And always remembering that:

- Faith and love working together springs forth Hope.
- Hope is what fuels our lives as Christians.
- It is what prepares us for those difficult times in life, even times that might include death.
- It is what gives us courage and allows us to overcome fear.
- Hope is so powerful, nothing can break it, not even death.

Let us pray,

Jesus, I trust in You! Amen.

Day 44

Mentoring

A wise person once shared that we should always be mentoring someone while at the same time being a mentee of someone else. What a wonderful ideology. As a mentor, we can share with the willing participant the wisdom learned from our successes and our failures. As we mentee, we are able to benefit as the recipient of the advice and wisdom of one who has experienced more than us or who has the enhanced wisdom and understanding to see things more clearly than maybe we can. Being a mentor also has a charitable aspect in the sense that we can unselfishly give to another what has been gifted to us. Specifically, our experiences and the insights gained usually are a result of God's grace and knowing that all knowledge originates in and from God. So, as it has been given to us, we can pass it on to another as a gift in the same fashion that it had been gifted to us. As a mentee, we can further develop our humility in realizing that we do not have all the answers and in fact, there are many more people in the world more learned, wise, and capable of better understanding the complexities in life than many of us.

Many years ago, in our culture, there were extended families living together that included grandparents. Having the ability to daily speak to one who had journeyed through many years of life so enriched the members of the family. Not only could you obtain sage advice so easily it was usually combined with sincere love and care, being that it was coming from a member of the same family. These same individuals, the patriarchs and matriarchs of the families, were also often the spiritual leaders of the families. Wisdom and faith so often go hand in hand. Could it be that the devil had something to do with the splitting apart of families? Divide and concur has been a war term and strategy for the earliest of times, could it be a strategic plan for the devil too. By the separation and removal of grandparents, the devil was able to make access to their wisdom and spirituality much more difficult to acquire. Often our faith is enriched by trials and times of difficulty. It was these grandparents who had endured such trials and difficulties and come through a better person because of it. Something to consider, especially if you have children in the home. How involved in your life are the grandparents? Even if you do not have children in the home. How often are you connecting with your parents? Even if your parents have passed on, are you praying to them and asking for them to intercede for you and to help you from heaven?

EXERCISE – Identify below who has been your mentor and who has been your mentee.

Who in your life has been a mentor to you?

1. _____
2. _____
3. _____

Who have you been a mentor for?

1. _____
2. _____
3. _____

Let us pray,

Ever loving Lord,

Assist us in our efforts to receive guidance from others, living our true humility, and give us the patience and ability to gracefully mentor others in the way that you had humbled yourself to come to earth in human form to be our mentor showing us the way, the truth, and life.

Amen.

Use this section below to journal any thoughts or inspirations from the meditation to help with further reflection.

_____
_____
_____
_____
_____
_____

Day 45

Intellectual and Personal Growth

There is one day in life that we can finally say that we have learned enough and that there is no further need for study and growth. That day will be the day that we die. Since it is upon our death that the beatific vision is revealed to us and we will be able to see life as God had seen it, without the restraints and restriction of our human vails. We will understand why things occurred and we will be able to see all the ripple effects of those events. Even the most tragic of circumstance will now be understood in the light of God's grace. We will also be able to see how one's inactions affected us and those around us as well. Everything will suddenly make sense, and there will no longer be any unanswered questions.

Yet, for now, we do not have that beatific vision and we only have our human intellect available to us. It is desirous for us to continually learn about life, love, God, and the human and spiritual conditions. We should be engaged in this learning process. How to do this is the discerning question. Some of us like to learn in a more social setting in groups and classes, while others enjoy private reading and study. The how isn't as important as the what we are learning. A stagnant mind becomes weak and frail, while a mind exercised continues to be strong and resilient.

Learning can be fun and exciting, and sometimes it can be less stimulating but still quite rewarding and even necessary. Ask yourself these questions, how is it that I am still intellectually and personally growing? What have I intentionally added to my life to provide for intellectual and personal growth?

As is has been mentioned before, the most difficult step in creating change is taking the first step. Once that step is taken then a movement has begun. Think about what that first step might be for you in respect to creating a life of perpetual learning and feeding and nourishing of your intellect.

EXERCISE

What are three things in life that interest you?

1. _____
2. _____
3. _____

What can you do to begin or enhance the process of intellectual and personal growth in your life?

1. _____
2. _____
3. _____

Let us pray,

Dear almighty God,

knowing our inner most thoughts and desires,

provide for us the insight necessary to know what aspects of our lives You wish for us to develop further.

We also humbly ask that you guide our thoughts and decisions to make the right choices and to feel encouraged and motivated to continually grow in ways that will be pleasing to you.

Amen.

Use this section below to journal any thoughts or inspirations from the meditation to help with further reflection.

Day 46

Leaven

"To what shall I compare the Kingdom of God?
It is like yeast that a woman took
and mixed in with three measures of wheat flour
until the whole batch of dough was leavened."
Luke 13:20-21

Have you given much thought to what our actions should look like in the world as Christians? If so, you are in good company since there are hundreds if not thousands of holy people who have done just the same over the centuries. Jesus speaks to the Kingdom of God and uses the parable of yeast and leaven bread which many have found to mean that we are to be that leaven in the world.

What is leaven? When someone was making bread in the first century, they'd throw in a little piece of dough that was held over from the last time they made bread. By this time that dough would have fermented and become leaven. When leaven was added to a new batch of bread, it would act like yeast, causing the bread to rise.

What did Jesus mean by this parable? Well, we might consider that He was speaking to the growth of the kingdom of heaven in the individual heart and in the world at large, because:

- its source is from without;
- it is secret in its operation;
- it spreads by contact of particle with particle;
- it is widely diffusive, one particle of leaven being able to change any number of particles of flour;

- and because it does not act like water, moistening a certain amount of flour, but is like a plant, changing the particles it comes in contact with into its own nature, with like propagating power

Can you see a correlation to how this might be a directive and guide to us in our lives and how our actions, behaviors, and how we interact with others could be used as leaven in this world we live in?

CHALLENGE - Take a minute now and throughout this day reflect upon how the Kingdom of Heaven could be leavened from within you, and also how you could be like holy yeast leavening the people and circumstances around you.

Let us pray,

The light of God surrounds me,
the love of God enfolds me,
the power of God protects me,
the presence of God watches over me,
wherever I am, God is,
and where God is, all is perfect.
Amen.

Use this section below to journal any thoughts or inspirations from the meditation to help with further reflection.

Day 47

The Angelus Prayer

To be holy also means that we are united with God in our thoughts and behaviors. Living in the secular world we can so often be drawn away and distracted from thinking about God and the heavenly world. The Angelus prayer is a wonderful way to reconnect in prayer three set times per day at 6 a.m., noon, and 6 p.m.

Designed to commemorate the mystery of the Incarnation and pay homage to Mary's role in salvation history, it has long been part of Catholic life. Around the world, three times every day, the faithful stop whatever they are doing and with the words "The Angel of the Lord declared unto Mary" to begin this simple yet beautiful prayer.

This devotion reminds us of the Angel Gabriel's annunciation to Mary, Mary's fiat, the Incarnation and Our Lord's passion and resurrection. It is repeated as a holy invitation, calling us to prayer and meditation. Over the years many of the faithful have focused the morning Angelus on the Resurrection, the noon Angelus on the Passion, and the evening Angelus on the Incarnation.

It is said that over the centuries workers in the fields halted their labors and prayed when they heard the Angelus bell. This pious practice is depicted by Jean-François Millet's famous 1857 painting (above) which shows two workers in a potato field stopping to say the Angelus. There are also stories that animals would automatically stop plowing and stand quietly at the bell.

Like a heavenly messenger, the Angelus calls man to interrupt his daily, earthly routines and turn to thoughts of God, of the Blessed Mother, and of eternity. As Pope Benedict XVI taught on the feast of the Annunciation: "The Angel's proclamation was addressed to her; she accepted it, and when she responded from the depths of her heart … at that moment the eternal Word began to exist as a human being in time. From generation to generation the wonder evoked by this ineffable mystery never ceases."

V. The Angel of the Lord declared unto Mary.

R. And she conceived of the Holy Spirit.

Hail Mary, full of grace,

The Lord is with Thee;

Blessed art thou among women,

And blessed is the fruit of thy womb, Jesus.

Holy Mary, Mother of God,

Pray for us sinners,

Now and at the hour of our death. Amen.

V. Behold the handmaid of the Lord.

R. Be it done unto me according to thy word.

Hail Mary, etc.

V. And the Word was made Flesh.

R. And dwelt among us.

Hail Mary, etc.

V. Pray for us, O holy Mother of God.

R. That we may be made worthy of the promises of Christ.

LET US PRAY,

Pour forth, we beseech Thee, O Lord, Thy grace into our hearts, that we to whom the Incarnation of Christ Thy Son was made known by the message of an angel, may by His Passion and Cross be brought to the glory of His Resurrection. Through the same Christ Our Lord.

Amen.

Day 48

So many people give great attention to the Commandments, however, they seem to neglect or all together misunderstand the significance of the Second Commandment. God felt that this was so important that He created a commandment, a law, for us. As you may recall, these Commandments have been gifted to us so that we may be free to live life to the fullest and to help us journey toward everlasting life in heaven. So, let's take a few minutes to gain a greater understanding of the significance of this Commandment.

You shall not take the name of the Lord your God in vain.

The Second Commandment prescribes respect for the Lord's name. Like the First Commandment, it belongs to the virtue of religion and more particularly it governs our use of speech in sacred matters. Among all the words of Revelation, there is one which is unique: the revealed name of God. God confides his name to those who believe in him; he reveals himself to them in his personal mystery. The gift of a name belongs to the order of trust and intimacy. "The Lord's name is holy." For this reason, man must not abuse it. He must keep it in mind in silent, loving adoration. He will not introduce it into his own speech except to bless, praise, and glorify it. Respect for his name is an expression of the respect owed to the mystery of God himself and to the whole sacred reality it evokes. The sense of the sacred is part of the virtue of religion.

The Second Commandment forbids the abuse of God's name, i.e., every improper use of the names of God, Jesus Christ, but also of the Virgin Mary and all the saints. Promises made to others in God's name engage the divine honor, fidelity, truthfulness, and authority. They must be respected in justice. To be unfaithful to them is to misuse God's name and in some way to make God out to be a liar.

Blasphemy is directly opposed to the Second Commandment. It consists in uttering against God - inwardly or outwardly - words of hatred, reproach, or defiance; in speaking ill of God; in failing in respect toward him in one's speech; in misusing God's name. St. James condemns those "who blaspheme that honorable name [of Jesus] by which you are called." The prohibition of blasphemy extends to language against Christ's Church, the saints, and sacred things. It is also blasphemous to make use of God's name to cover up criminal practices, to reduce peoples to servitude, to torture persons or put them to death. The misuse of God's name to commit a crime can provoke others to repudiate religion. Blasphemy is contrary to the respect due God and his holy name. It is in itself a grave sin. Catechism of the Catholic Church, # 2142-2148.

EXERCISE – Take a minute to reflect upon your speech and the use of God, Jesus, Mary, the Saints, etc. Is it always done with great reverence and respect? How do we use the Lord's name? Is it only used to bless, praise, and glorify it? Did we realize that speaking against Christ's Church, the saints, and sacred things is also considered blasphemy? Have I ever committed sin against the Second Commandment?

Let us pray,

Most glorious Virgin Mary, Mother of God and our Mother, turn thine eyes in pity upon us, miserable sinners; we are sorely afflicted by the many evils that surround us in this life, but especially do we feel our hearts break within us upon hearing the dreadful insults and blasphemies uttered against thee, O Virgin Immaculate. O how these impious sayings offend the infinite Majesty of God and of His only-begotten Son, Jesus Christ! How they provoke His indignation and give us cause to fear the terrible effects of His vengeance! Would that the sacrifice of our lives might avail to put an end to such outrages and blasphemies; were it so, how gladly we should make it, for we desire, O most holy Mother, to love thee and to honor thee with all our hearts, since this is the will of God. And just because we love thee, we will do all that is in our power to make thee honored and loved by all men. In the meantime, do thou, our merciful Mother, the supreme comforter of the afflicted, accept this our act of reparation which we offer thee for ourselves and for all our families, as well as for all who impiously blaspheme thee, not knowing what they say. Do thou obtain for them from Almighty God the grace of conversion, and thus render more manifest and more glorious thy kindness, thy power, and thy great mercy. May they join with us in proclaiming thee blessed among women, the Immaculate Virgin and most compassionate Mother of God. Amen.

Day 49

Intentional Acts of Kindness

The world is full of self-centered, self-absorbed, and narcissistic-like people. We might even be one of them if we are honest enough to admit it. Maybe that is one of the reasons why we chose to participate in the *100 days to Freedom* program, to learn to live outside of ourselves and to gain a better appreciation of those around us. Maybe through God's grace, at one point in our life, He allowed and maybe even inspired us to see just a glimpse of this self-centeredness within us. These ever so often revelations of our inadequacies are sometimes just what we need to wake-up and to feel inspired to make a change.

The more one does something in life, especially things that are intentional, the more they become a natural part of our lives and often an essential part of who we are. By directing our attention and efforts toward intentional acts of kindness shifts the focus from us to someone else. It is impossible to be thinking of someone else and ourselves at the same time. Specifically, thinking about how I could be nice and charitable to a particular person prevents me from thinking about myself, at least at that moment. The more we think about serving others, trying to be kind to others, and looking for even the slightest opportunity to brighten or lighten another person's day, radically adjusts our thinking and behaviors from being self-serving and self-centered to thoughts of being charitable and loving.

Intentional acts of kindness often require no money, no preplanning, and no exceptional effort. What it does take is the mindset that one will keep an open mind and heart, be observant of the needs of others, and then using some creativity in how one could assist with an act of generosity, kindness, understanding, compassion, and love. One might be surprised that when this shift occurs and one stops looking inward but instead looks outward, just how many opportunities God places in their lives to make a difference in another person's life.

EXERCISE – Please take a minute and think about a few situations that might have recently been revealed to you, and then what you could have done as an intentional act of kindness,

Situation	Potential Intentional Act of Kindness
1.	1.
2.	2.
3.	3.
4.	4.

Let us pray,

O Lord God, I love you above all things
and I love my neighbor for your sake
because you are the highest, infinite and perfect good,
worthy of all my love.
In this love I intend to live and die.
Amen.

Use this section below to journal any thoughts or inspirations from the meditation to help with further reflection.

_____
_____
_____
_____
_____
_____

Day 50

Mealtime Prayers

As we continue with our journey with the *100 days to Freedom* most of us should be gaining an appreciation for food in a different way than we had experienced if before. If we have been obedient to the discipline of fasting, the sin of Gluttony has probably become more apparent in our lives. As it has been said before, seeing things in a degree of contrast often helps us to see things more clearly. Having days of fasting alternating with days of eating can help to bring balance and perspective to us. The other almost automatic benefit of fasting is that when one does eat after the completed fast, food seems to be even more flavorful and delightful.

Even though the discipline of fasting is self-initiated, it can take on a deeper sense of obligation when it is connected at a deeper level such as with a promise or oath to God and can be used as a means of prayerful self-sacrifice for others and for the reparation for past sins. Then after the breaking of the fast, as intended and structured, food can be seen as a reward or gift from God. It is in these gifts that we can and should give thanks to God for the blessings that he has bestowed upon us.

The ordinary way we give thanks to God before the consumption of a meal is by prayer. One of the most popular meal blessings is as follows:

Bless us, O Lord! and these Thy gifts,

which we are about to receive

from Thy bounty, through Christ our Lord.

Amen.

It would not seem right or proper to receive a gift from someone and then run away without saying thank you. The same is true for the gift of a meal. Additionally, as Christians, we should always have in the forefront of our minds the needs of others and to pray for those who have less than we do. Again, this ideology supports the desire to think of others before ourselves and to love our neighbor as ourselves. A traditional after-meal prayer is as follows:

> **We give Thee thanks for all Thy benefits, O Almighty God,**
> **who livest and reignest world without end.**
> **Amen.**
> **May the souls of the faithful departed,**
> **through the mercy of God, rest in peace.**
> **Amen.**

As Christians, we are to also keep in mind that those who have departed from this earth often need a time of purification prior to entrance into the heavenly kingdom where no sin, or evil thought or deed, or even a remnant of such shall be present. This process of purification is timeless since it is a spiritual process and the soul of the individual has already separated from the body and is not constrained by time and space. So, to think of this time in "Purgatory" where past sins are purged from the soul, and the soul is purified, as a specific place or location would not be adequate, but rather as a process. It is within this process that the soul is no longer able to pray for itself but NEEDS the prayers of others to help with the reception of God's mercy. This great need must not be overlooked and forgotten and that is why our prayer after meals includes the mention of the souls of the faithful departed.

CHALLENGE – Try to begin today the discipline of praying before every meal and then also offering a prayer of thankfulness after each meal. This will quickly become a habit in your life, a new holy habit.

Use this section below to journal any thoughts or inspirations from the meditation to help with further reflection.

100 days to Freedom

Day 51

It is never too late

Often people fall into despair when they begin their journey of Christianity. As God gifts them with insight into the way of life, true life, and Jesus' messages of the Kingdom of God, they also begin to see the contrast of their past actions and behaviors in this new light of clarity. It is upon this refection of just how sinful one had been, that thoughts of it maybe being too late can surface and subsequently bring despair and doubt. Yet, one only needs to look to the Gospels for reassurance that it is never too late to come to Christ.

At that time, Jesus came to Jericho and intended to pass through the town.
Now a man there named Zacchaeus,
who was a chief tax collector and also a wealthy man,
was seeking to see who Jesus was;
but he could not see him because of the crowd,
for he was short in stature.

So he ran ahead and climbed a sycamore tree in order to see Jesus,
who was about to pass that way.
When he reached the place, Jesus looked up and said,
"Zacchaeus, come down quickly,
for today I must stay at your house."
And he came down quickly and received him with joy.

When they all saw this, they began to grumble, saying,
"He has gone to stay at the house of a sinner."
But Zacchaeus stood there and said to the Lord,
"Behold, half of my possessions, Lord, I shall give to the poor,
and if I have extorted anything from anyone
I shall repay it four times over."

**And Jesus said to him,
"Today salvation has come to this house
because this man, too, is a descendant of Abraham.
For the Son of Man has come to seek
and to save what was lost."
Luke 19: 1-10**

Clearly, it is never too late to change our ways and to begin living a life of honesty, charity, faith, and love. Saint Luke reiterates just how possible it is to turn back to God and to experience the overwhelming spirit of joy awaiting the repentant.

**I tell you,
in just the same way
there will be more joy in heaven
over one sinner who repents than over ninety-nine
righteous people who have no need of repentance.**

Luke 15:7

Let us pray,

*Loving Father, you are the source of all goodness and love, and you
never refuse forgiveness to those who come to you with repentant hearts.
Mercifully listen to my prayer.*

*Look with kindness upon me and forgive me for all my sins and failures.
Give me the grace to acknowledge them before you.
Help me to look into my life and see the many ways I have displeased
you in my relationship with you, with my loved ones and friends,
through the sin of pride, the sin of anger, lust or weakness of the flesh, envy,
greed, gluttony, and sloth and for all the negative consequences that resulted from them.*

*Forgive me for my inability to be faithful to your commandments.
And bless me with humility to repent with a sincere and contrite heart.
Give me the strength to fight future temptations to sin and to
avoid being exposed to occasions for sin.
Give me the patience and perseverance to make amends in my life
and be transformed as you will.*

All these I pray in Jesus' name through Mary and all the angels and saints. Amen.

Day 52

Happiness

How many of us feel that to be normal means that we are to be happy? And to be happy, does this mean every day, every other day, most of the time? Does it mean that if we experience days where we are not happy then are we not normal? What is happiness by the way, is there a definition? The dictionary defines happiness as a state of well-being and contentment. So, what is well-being? The dictionary defines it as a state of being happy, healthy, and prosperous. Well, what if one doesn't feel happy? Does that mean they're not healthy? Does that mean they are not to be prosperous? Is all doomed? That doesn't seem to be true.

For most, happiness is a word that is difficult to understand when it comes right down to it. Many could be content with the feeling of peacefulness and fulfillment in life. Yet, to have fulfillment one usually needs to have an understanding of what it is they need to fulfill or complete. What is it in life that one strives for that will not leave them still lacking once obtained? Often the answers to life's questions have already been answered, we just need to know where to look. For some, they look forward while seeking something new, while others have the wisdom to look backward to the truths that are well-tested and tried. The old Baltimore Catechism has many of these life's answers so clearly identified. Here are just a few examples:

1. Who made us?

God made us.

2. Who is God?

God is the Supreme Being, infinitely perfect, who made all things and keeps them in existence.

3. Why did God make us?

God made us to show forth His goodness and to share with us His everlasting happiness in heaven.

4. What must we do to gain the happiness of heaven?

To gain the happiness of heaven we must know, love, and serve God in this world.

5. From whom do we learn to know, love, and serve God?

We learn to know, love, and serve God from Jesus Christ, the Son of God, who teaches us through the Catholic Church.

6. Where do we find the chief truths taught by Jesus Christ through the Catholic Church?

We find the chief truths taught by Jesus Christ through the Catholic Church in the Apostles' Creed.

7. Say the Apostles' Creed.

I believe in God, the Father Almighty, Creator of heaven and earth; and in Jesus Christ, His only Son, Our Lord; who was conceived by the Holy Spirit, born of the Virgin Mary, suffered under Pontius Pilate, was crucified, died and was buried. He descended into hell; the third day He arose again from the dead; He ascended into heaven, sits at the right hand of God, the Father Almighty; from there He shall come to judge the living and the dead. I believe in the Holy Spirit, the Holy Catholic Church, the communion of Saints, the forgiveness of sins, the resurrection of the body, and life everlasting. Amen.

To be happy, peaceful, or content has much more to do with understanding who it is that is Happiness, Peacefulness, and Love. That person is God who is known to us as the Holy Trinity: Father, Son, and Holy Spirit. To know God is to know happiness, peacefulness, and true content in life. This journey through *100 days to Freedom* will help us to grow in intimacy with God through the disciplines and with God's grace.

Let us pray,

Lord, take my heart on a journey, Into your goodness and grace. Where I walk on grass soft with forgiveness and wait by the everlasting lake. Lord, take my mind to a new place filled with the promise of life. Where I rest with great dreams of your kingdom and wake with a new joy inside. Lord, take my soul to adventure may I find greater freedom in you. Where I run with great vision and insight and trust that my dreams are from you. Lord, take me into your promise where eternity awaits at the door. And I find I'm renewed, redeemed and restored Oh Jesus, I'm alive now for you! Amen.

Day 53

How to live one's life

Many people find it difficult to know how it is to live one's life. There are so many influences and influencers out there in the world teaching and preaching so many different ideologies and methods that on the surface seem to make so much sense until they are actually attempted, and the user is left still wanting more. Saint Paul in his letter to the Romans has some inspired advice that appears to not only speak of the truth but appears to be still relevant to us today.

Brothers and sisters:
We, though many, are one body in Christ
and individually parts of one another.
Since we have gifts that differ according to the grace given to us,
let us exercise them:
if prophecy, in proportion to the faith;
if ministry, in ministering;
if one is a teacher, in teaching;
if one exhorts, in exhortation;
if one contributes, in generosity;
if one is over others, with diligence;
if one does acts of mercy, with cheerfulness.

Let love be sincere;
hate what is evil,
hold on to what is good;

love one another with mutual affection;

anticipate one another in showing honor.

Do not grow slack in zeal,

be fervent in spirit,

serve the Lord.

Rejoice in hope,

endure in affliction,

persevere in prayer.

Contribute to the needs of the holy ones,

exercise hospitality.

Bless those who persecute you,

bless and do not curse them.

Rejoice with those who rejoice,

weep with those who weep.

Have the same regard for one another;

do not be haughty but associate with the lowly.

CHALLENGE: Reflect upon Saint Paul's words and directives. Take a moment to see how these words hold up against your life. Does your life reflect Saint's Paul's words? Are there opportunities for some change or adjustment in the way you think and act in life? Identifying opportunities in our lives is the first step to enacting meaningful change.

Use this section below to journal any thoughts or inspirations from the meditation to help with further reflection.

_____

_____

_____

_____

_____

Day 54

Remember to keep holy the Sabbath day

The Third Commandment to remember to keep holy the sabbath day is probably one of the most neglected commandments that God has given to us. The Catechism of the Catholic Church explains the significance of the Commandment as follows.

God's action is the model for human action. If God "rested and was refreshed" on the seventh day, man too ought to "rest" and should let others, especially the poor, "be refreshed." The sabbath brings everyday work to a halt and provides a respite. It is a day of protest against the servitude of work and the worship of money.

The Sunday celebration of the Lord's Day and his Eucharist is at the heart of the Church's life. "Sunday is the day on which the Paschal mystery is celebrated in light of the apostolic tradition and is to be observed as the foremost Holy Day of Obligation in the universal Church."

This practice of the Christian assembly dates from the beginnings of the apostolic age. The Letter to the Hebrews reminds the faithful "not to neglect to meet together, as is the habit of some, but to encourage one another."

Tradition preserves the memory of an ever-timely exhortation: Come to Church early, approach the Lord, and confess your sins, repent in prayer. . . . Be present at the sacred and divine liturgy, conclude its prayer and do not leave before the dismissal. . . . We have often said: "This day is given to you for prayer and rest. This is the day that the Lord has made, let us rejoice and be glad in it."

Just as God "rested on the seventh day from all his work which he had done," human life has a rhythm of work and rest. The institution of the Lord's Day helps everyone enjoy adequate rest and leisure to cultivate their familial, cultural, social, and religious lives.

Those Christians who have leisure should be mindful of their brethren who have the same needs and the same rights yet cannot rest from work because of poverty and misery. Sunday is traditionally consecrated by Christian piety to good works and humble service of the sick, the infirm, and the elderly.

Christians will also sanctify Sunday by devoting time and care to their families and relatives, often difficult to do on other days of the week. Sunday is a time for reflection, silence, cultivation of the mind, and meditation which furthers the growth of the Christian interior life.

EXERCISE – List five ways you keep your sabbath holy.

1. _____
2. _____
3. _____
4. _____
5. _____

Let us pray,

Gracious and holy Father,
grant us the intellect to understand You,
reason to discern You, diligence to seek You,
wisdom to find You, a spirit to know You,
a heart to meditate upon You.
May our ears hear You, may our eyes behold You,
and may our tongues proclaim You.
Give us grace that our way of life may be pleasing to You,
that we may have the patience to wait for You
and the perseverance to look for You.
Grant us a perfect end - Your holy presence,
a blessed resurrection and life everlasting.
We ask this through Jesus Christ our Lord. Amen.

Day 55

Discernment

It is not very difficult to choose between good and evil, good and bad, right versus wrong, but when the choices in life are not so clear as previously mentioned, then making the proper choice can be troublesome and difficult. The most frequent question presented in spiritual direction is "How do I know if I am making the right decision?" This is even more complicated when it has to do with making a choice between two options, both appearing to be good and to have merit. How does one know what to choose?

In discernment, a person is to be reminded that the goal is to be following God's will and His unique plan for them. It is helpful to reflect deeply on who God created us to be prior to making big life decisions. As previously mentioned in the *100 days to Freedom* journey, God has been forming us from the very beginning to grow more profoundly into the specific and unique being that we are. He has gifted us with special talents, abilities, and aptitudes to fulfill His mission, our mission. It is through the trials, temptations, successes, failures, and even our own sinfulness that God uses it all, everything, to mold us in a perpetual growth to become the best version of ourselves that we can imagine. God patiently allows this growth to occur and delights as we become more and more united with Him.

The discernment process should always be grounded in prayer, the way we communicate with God. We should ask for guidance and reassurance in making our decisions in life. We should never neglect to ask for the Holy Spirit to provide wisdom and insight into the decision-making process as well as using those around us to discuss and evaluate the potential repercussions and ramifications of the choices laid before us. The devil would love for us to keep things hidden, isolated, and removed from others. This is where he uses his power of temptation and allurement to foster such things as greed, pride, envy, etc.

As we openly share our discernment options with others and we bring those options out into the light, the devil loses his power on persuasion since he prefers to work in the dark, in secret, tempting, and teasing.

Making big and small decisions are part of everyday life. As long as we keep the discernment process focused on supporting our unique plan and path in life, we will usually be successful in making the proper choices. We must remember, however, even if we do make the improper choice, God will use that, too, to help develop virtue, faith, and love in our lives.

As we make life decisions we should always ask, what choice will honor God the most, and what choice will help me along my path of knowing God better, serving God better, and helping me to grow closer to Him whom I should love above all things.

Let us pray,

O Lord God,

I have no idea where I am going, I do not see the road ahead of me,

I cannot know for certain where it will end.

Nor do I really know myself,

and that fact that I think I am following Your will does not mean that I am actually doing so.

But I believe that the desire to please You does, in fact, please You.

And I hope I have that desire in all that I am doing.

I hope that I will never do anything apart from that desire to please You.

And I know that if I do this You will lead me by the right road,

though I may know nothing about it.

Therefore, I will trust You always though I may seem to be lost and in the shadow of death.

I will not fear,

for You are ever with me,

And You will never leave me to make my journey alone. Amen.

Day 56

Congratulations, you have made it to day 56 (8 weeks). This is a good time to stop, take a deep breath, and to evaluate how well, or maybe how not so well, the disciplines are going. Please take a minute, break out a pen or pencil, and complete this very important self-evaluation regarding adherence.

Spiritual	1 No Action	2 Almost none	3 Hit and miss	4 Almost perfect	5 Nailed it!
Daily Mass or Daily Mass readings and Spiritual Communion					
Daily Rosary					
Formal Examination of Conscience nightly					
Daily Spiritual reading					
Weekly adoration in front of the Blessed Sacrament					
Monthly Confession					

Physical	1 No Action	2 Almost none	3 Hit and miss	4 Almost perfect	5 Nailed it!
Walk or Run daily					
Push-ups / Sit-ups / Lunges daily or weight lifting					
Stretches daily					
7-8 hours' sleep a night					

Nutrition	1 No Action	2 Almost none	3 Hit and miss	4 Almost perfect	5 Nailed it!
2-3 meals a day - No eating between meals					
No candy / desserts					
No fast-food					
Fasting on Mon / Wed / Friday					

Self-Denial	1 No Action	2 Almost none	3 Hit and miss	4 Almost perfect	5 Nailed it!
No major purchases (Toiletries and needed items only)					
No TV or movies					
No social media					
No Alcohol					

Well, how did you do? Let me guess, maybe less than perfect? Join the club, I have yet to meet the perfect human or the one who completed the entire *100 days to Freedom* program without missing a discipline even once. That makes you normal, human, and maybe a little less than a superhero. Yet, as Christians, we are called toward a path of perfection, a life of holiness, a life in which we journey closer and closer to God.

The structure of this program will allow each of us to grow, to grow in virtue, character, self-discipline, and in relationship with God. Reflect once again on the scores you gave yourself above and then on the categories: Spiritual Life, Physical Health, Nutritional Health, and Self-Discipline. If you identify an area where there is more opportunity for growth, then try to place a greater focus on that area for the next week.

We have all been created in God's image and likeness, and we have been created as unique individuals. No two journeys are alike, just like no two scorecards are exactly alike. God is working in us in the exact way He feels that He needs to work in us to help us to travel our unique journey. Let go and allow Him to drive this journey. Our part is to be open to His promptings and respond when He calls.

Keep up the good work and as you progress day-by-day be prepared to enjoy the rewards that God has ready for you. Whenever we turn our focus away from ourselves and upon the Lord, we begin to realize what freedom truly feels and looks like.

Let us pray,

Father, look upon our weakness and reach out to help us with Your loving power.
You redeem us and make us Your children in Christ.
Look upon us, give us true freedom and bring us to the inheritance You promised.
We ask this through our Lord Jesus Christ, Your Son,
who lives and reigns with You and the Holy Spirit,
one God, forever and ever. Amen.

Day 57

Clean on the inside

For so many of us, it has become a routine and habit to shower or bathe on a daily basis to keep our bodies clean and without odor or stain of dirt. This daily grooming and care of our hygiene assists with improving our appearance and attractiveness. Have you ever thought about what you do for your internal hygiene? What is it that you do to cleanse your inside? Our thoughts can become stained with negativity, with impurities, and also with the darkness of sin. Our souls can absorb this ugliness and over time can become quite remarkably tarnished.

Once we realize that we have neglected our inner cleanliness the first thing we should do is to address it with haste. Bring to light and to the forefront of our minds what it is that has darkened our souls and our intellect and ask God to help in the cleansing process.

Heavenly Father,
I come before You today, requesting that You cleanse me of anything that breaks Your heart.
Purify my mind, body, and soul.
Help me to seek righteousness above all else and not stray into the temptations of the world.
Save me from that unclean spirit, wash me in the precious blood to make me white as snow.
Remove what's dark in me and replace it with the good.
Set my paths straight, Oh Merciful Savior!
Amen!

As for mortal sin, those of the 10 Commandments and those of serious and grave circumstance, we need the power of Holy Confession/Reconciliation to be reunited with God and to receive the grace not only to cleanse our soul appropriately but to have the fortitude to fight against further and repeated sin in our lives.

How else does one keep their insides clean and holy and pure? We need to frequently and routinely cleanse it with the word of God through the reading of His inspired word in the Scripture. All Christians should develop a routine of reading daily Scripture. As you have noticed by participating in the *100 days to Freedom* program, each day includes the reading of the daily readings which includes Scripture from the Old Testament, the psalms, and the New Testament. This discipline is a minimal habit to fuel our day, but is not exclusive of the desired or necessary Scripture reading that we may need. We should find great comfort, direction, and guidance as we turn to Scripture and meditate on the inspired words of the Bible. The key to Scripture reading is to meditate and reflect upon the words and find their deeper meaning as they relate to living our lives. It is in this contemplation that we not only find clarity, inspiration, and surety in our lives, but we are simultaneously cleansed internally from those negative things that can creep inside of our thoughts and minds. If we are feeding our insides with things that are good and pure, healthy and honest, then there is little room for those things which are not good and pure and are not healthy and honest.

Like a car, garage, a pantry, or a house that is kept clean, it isn't something we do every once in a while, it is in the daily attention, effort, and work that is done that ensures the perpetual desired presentation. The same is true of our inner thoughts and for our souls. It is in the daily attention, effort, and work that allows our minds to be pure, clean, and positive. The same is true for our souls, by feeding it things that are holy, true, and honest, we will become those things in the same.

Use this section below to journal any thoughts or inspirations from the meditation to help with further reflection.

_____

_____

_____

_____

_____

_____

_____

_____

_____

Day 58

Faith, Hope, Love and Death

How often in our lives to do we talk about our death, or the end of our life with those around us, especially those close to us like our spouses, family, and friends? It is much easier to talk about the death of others than it is to talk about our own death.

As Christians, we are to be living our lives in preparation for death. A life well-lived, especially in regard to a life well-lived in the faith, brings about a comfortable death and ease of transition from this life to the next. But why is it that so many people fear death? Fear of death comes from a lack of faith and hope. Faith is the foundation of our spiritual life that we are to have as Christians, and it is with this faith that brings us hope. It is that hope that brings us courage in the light of difficulty, even when that difficulty includes the possibility of death. That hope is the understanding that there will be life after death, a life of such love, peace, and tranquility like we have never seen or experienced before.

So how does this all come about? Like many things in life, it begins in the family. The Father brings faith and truth into the home. Not exclusively, but that is his role and task. The wife embraces that faith and truth, internalizes it, and turns it into love and charity. It is the wife who is the heart and love of the home. And when the father who is faith, mixes with the wife who is love, working together, springs forth hope. With faith and hope, we are able to combat fear. The fear of death is only present when we are lacking faith and hope in our lives. Especially because it is faith and hope that specifically brings forth courage.

At this point, you might be asking how is it that we can embrace our Christian lives, our Catholic faith, be living our lives well, and how we can be prepared for when difficult times come, especially times that might involve death. First of all, we are to do the basics of what it means to be Catholic.

- We are to speak and listen to God daily in prayer.
- We are to attend weekly Mass and Holy Days of Obligation.
- We should cleanse our soul quickly every time it becomes stained with mortal sin through the Sacrament of confession.
- We are to be charitable with our time, talents, and treasure.
- We are to learn our faith and especially what the Church teaches about death so that we are well prepared to make the right decisions for ourselves and for our loved ones.

Also, we are always to remember that:

- Our Faith, truly understood and truly lived brings us hope.
- Faith mixed with love springs forth hope.
- Hope is what fuels our lives as Christians.
    - It is what prepares us for those difficult times in life, even times that might include death.
    - It is what gives us courage and allows us to overcome fear.

Catholic hope is so powerful, so truly powerful, nothing can break it, not even death. Amen.

Use this section below to journal any thoughts or inspirations from the meditation to help with further reflection.

_____
_____
_____
_____
_____
_____
_____
_____
_____
_____

Day 59

Honor thy Father and Mother

(From the Catechism of the Catholic Church)

Being numbered fourth in the order of the Commandments shows us the order of charity. God has willed that, after Him, we should honor our parents to whom we owe life and who have handed on to us the knowledge of God. We are obliged to honor and respect all those whom God, for our good, has vested with his authority.

The Fourth Commandment is addressed expressly to children in their relationship with their father and mother because this relationship is the most universal. It likewise concerns the ties of kinship between members of the extended family. It requires honor, affection, and gratitude toward elders and ancestors. Finally, it extends to the duties of pupils to teachers, employees to employers, subordinates to leaders, citizens to their country, and to those who administer or govern it.

Observing the Fourth Commandment brings its reward: "Honor your father and your mother, that your days may be long in the land which the LORD your God gives you." Respecting this Commandment provides, along with spiritual fruits, temporal fruits of peace and prosperity. Conversely, failure to observe it brings great harm to communities and to individuals.

The divine fatherhood is the source of human fatherhood; this is the foundation of the honor owed to parents. The respect of children, whether minors or adults, for their father and mother is nourished by the natural affection born of the bond uniting them. It is required by God's Commandment.

Respect for parents (filial piety) derives from gratitude toward those who, by the gift of life, their love, and their work, have brought their children into the world and enabled them to grow in stature, wisdom, and grace. "With all your heart honor your father, and do not forget the birth pangs of your mother. Remember that through your parents you were born; what can you give back to them that equals their gift to you?"

Filial respect is shown by true docility and obedience. "My son, keep your father's Commandment, and forsake not your mother's teaching. When you walk, they will lead you; when you lie down, they will watch over you; and when you awake, they will talk with you." "A wise son hears his father's instruction, but a scoffer does not listen to rebuke."

As they grow up, children should continue to respect their parents. They should anticipate their wishes, willingly seek their advice, and accept their just admonitions. Obedience toward parents ceases with the emancipation of the children; not so respect, which is always owed to them. This respect has its roots in the fear of God, one of the gifts of the Holy Spirit.

The Fourth Commandment reminds grown children of their responsibilities toward their parents. As much as they can, they must give them material and moral support in old age and in times of illness, loneliness, or distress. Jesus recalls this duty of gratitude.

For the Lord honored the father above the children, and he confirmed the right of the mother over her sons. Whoever honors his father atones for sins, and whoever glorifies his mother is like one who lays up treasure. Whoever honors his father will be gladdened by his own children, and when he prays, he will be heard. Whoever glorifies his father will have a long life, and whoever obeys the Lord will refresh his mother.

Let us pray,

O my God,
I love Thee above all things with my whole heart and soul,
because Thou art all good and worthy of all love.
I also love my father and mother and wish to eternally honor and respect them.
I pray that You fill me with Your grace to see how I should and can honor my parents more fully and deeply in the way You command me.
Amen.

Day 60

Spiritual Reading

One of the disciplines in the *100 days to Freedom* journey is that of daily spiritual reading. Why is it that daily spiritual reading is so important? Have you ever heard the phrase, "We only know what we know? Well, that phrase speaks to us in the sense that we travel through life only knowing what we know. Yes, we do gain wisdom through experience and with encounters with others, but these experiences and encounters are not as numerous as one might imagine. We might have one significant encounter a day if we are blessed. However, having the ability to pick up a piece of writing from one of the Church's saints, or great spiritual writers, and learn and be exposed to their truths of life, love, friendship, and the virtues allow us to grow tremendously.

You might have noticed that a person who is well-read has usually acquired the ability to think and explore situations and events in a dynamic way. They have been exposed to a variety of attitudes and ideas through their reading and can assimilate those characteristics to their own way of thinking as well. However, it is important to choose wisely what we are reading, especially in the early stages of our formation, to ensure that we are being fed ideologies and truths consistent with our faith. As we grow in knowledge and our foundation has become more solidified, we can then be more adventurous with our literary choices since our discernment skills and critical thinking skills have developed more extensively.

In choosing not to develop the habit of daily spiritual reading is like choosing to ignore God's grace being gifted to us. God has allowed these holy and inspired men and women to document their thoughts, their received revelations, and their contemplations so that they can be shared with others. It is in the reception of these gifts that we are also receiving additional insight into who God is and even more importantly who God wants us to become. Ignoring this is like refusing a gift given to us from God.

In God's revelation He has offered us the words of the prophets, His only begotten son Jesus, the apostles, disciples, holy and learned men and women, and scholars and theologians, that can be so easily accessed in today's modern world to teach us and enlighten us. Yet, so many have chosen not to make any effort to experience them. Beginning with the very first proverb we hear how important it is to receive wise counsel and instruction.

> The proverbs of Solomon, the son of David, king of Israel:
> That people may know wisdom and discipline,
> may understand intelligent sayings;
> May receive instruction in wise conduct,
> in what is right, just and fair;
> That resourcefulness may be imparted to the naive,
> knowledge and discretion to the young.
> The wise by hearing them will advance in learning,
> the intelligent will gain sound guidance,
> To comprehend proverb and by word,
> the words of the wise and their riddles.
> Fear of the Lord is the beginning of knowledge;
> fools despise wisdom and discipline.

CHALLENGE – List two books or resources that you will begin reading today if you are not already doing so daily.

1. _____   2. _____

Let us pray,

O Mary, Mother of fair love, of fear, of knowledge, and of holy hope, by whose loving care and intercession many, otherwise poor in intellect, have wonderfully advanced in knowledge and in holiness, Thee do I choose as the guide and patroness of my studies; and I humbly implore, through the deep tenderness of Thy maternal love, and especially through that eternal Wisdom who deigned to take from Thee our flesh and who gifted Thee beyond all the saints with heavenly light, that Thou wouldst obtain for me by Thy intercession the grace of the Holy Spirit that I may be able to grasp with strong intellect, retain in memory, proclaim by word and deed, and teach others all things which bring honor to Thee and to Thy Son, and which for me and for others are salutary for eternal life. Amen.

Day 61

A Focused Purge

Now, well into the journey towards freedom you probably have noticed the many ways that you have grown in your spiritual and physical being. Having a daily discipline of prayer, exercise, self-denial, and proper eating, you have established routines and habits that will be life-lasting if you so choose to maintain them. You have probably also noticed that there are still one or two of your old habits that are still present and lingering in your life. These often tend to be things we are reluctant to give up or separate from for a variety of reasons, or we are still dependent upon them in some way. The other consideration is that the devil is using those last few things to remain connected and has given great effort to keep you shackled to them.

Day 61 is the day that we take a closer and deeper look at our lives and directly at those last remaining elements of sinfulness that are still lingering. It is time to break free and transition to the next level of holiness and to transform into the next stage of wholeness. Please take a minute and reflect on the following list to help with your discernment.

PRIDE: **Pride is undue self-esteem or self-love, which seeks attention and honor and sets oneself in competition with God.**

AVARICE: **(from Latin avarus, "greedy"; "to crave") is the inordinate love for riches. Its special malice, broadly speaking, lies in that it makes the getting and keeping of money, possessions, and the like, a purpose in itself to live for.**

ENVY: **Resentment or sadness at another's good fortune.**

WRATH: **The desire of vengeance.**

LUST:	**The inordinate craving for or indulgence in sexual pleasure.**
GLUTTONY:	**Overindulgence in food or drink. A glutton wants things too soon, too expensively, too much, too eagerly, too daintily.**
SLOTH:	**A culpable lack of physical or spiritual effort; acedia or laziness.**

Now that we have prayerfully, honestly, and openly contemplated our lives, our behaviors, our actions, and our lingering sinfulness, we are now prepared to offer to our Lord, through contrite hearts, our prayer asking for healing, strength, and fortitude against our habitual sinfulness. Please pray the following prayer.

Lord Jesus, forgive me.

I confess I have been offering myself over to sin, and now I am its slave.

I renounce it; I renounce my sins.

[Include in your prayer the things that you are still habitually doing]

I renounce every way I have given myself over to sin.

May your atoning blood cover my sins and cleanse me.

May your holiness possess me totally and completely.

Please forgive me and give me the strength to sin no more and to avoid all temptation.

Amen.

Now make plans to go to the Sacrament of confession as soon as possible.

Use this section below to journal any thoughts or inspirations from the meditation to help with further reflection.

_____

_____

_____

_____

Day 62

Joyful Service

How many of us are asked to do things that we don't really want to do? Not things that are wrong, dishonest, or even sinful, but tasks or duties that we would prefer not to do given the chance to decline. These types of things might be hosting an out of town friend at your home for a week, picking people up at the airport, visiting unfamiliar families over the holidays, etc. When we are faced with these dilemmas, we have two options to choose from in how we react. One option is to look for any excuse we can find to avoid them, the other is to embrace the task/duty with a joyful servant's heart and complete it to the best of our ability. When we choose the latter, we are choosing to serve the interests of others over our own interests. This self-sacrifice allows an opportunity for our hearts to grow, our pride and self-centeredness to shrink, and to elevate the dignity of others.

EXERCISE – Think of a few occurrences or situations where you were asked to do something that you did not want to do. How did you respond? What was the condition of your heart and mind as you did or did not do what was asked of you?

Situation	Response	Was I joyful and did I possess a servant's heart?

Galatians 5:13-14	For you were called for freedom, brothers. But do not use this freedom as an opportunity for the flesh; rather, serve one another through love. For the whole law is fulfilled in one statement, namely, "You shall love your neighbor as yourself."
Mark 25:35	For I was hungry and you gave me food, I was thirsty and you gave me drink, a stranger and you welcomed me.
Mathew 10:43-45	Rather, whoever wishes to be great among you will be your servant; whoever wishes to be first among you will be the slave of all. For the Son of Man did not come to be served but to serve and to give his life as a ransom for many.
1 Peter 4:8-11	Above all, let your love for one another be intense, because love covers a multitude of sins. Be hospitable to one another without complaining. As each one has received a gift, use it to serve one another as good stewards of God's varied grace. Whoever preaches, let it be with the words of God; whoever serves, let it be with the strength that God supplies, so that in all things God may be glorified through Jesus Christ, to whom belong glory and dominion forever and ever. Amen.

Use this section below to journal any thoughts or inspirations from the meditation to help with further reflection.

_____

_____

_____

_____

_____

_____

_____

_____

Day 63

Retreats

Why is it that so many say that taking a retreat once or twice a year is not only beneficial but a must for those on a spiritual journey? One might first respond and say that we work so hard and have so many responsibilities that we need time to unwind and to take time for just ourselves. But isn't that more of a vacation than a retreat? Others might say that a retreat is a time to separate ourselves from the world and give focused attention back to God. That response might be more accurate than the first, but it is still lacking in fullness.

A spiritual retreat has the qualities of refreshing and revitalizing by allowing opportunities for enhanced prayer, deep contemplation, and personal reflection of one's life especially in how it relates to God. A spiritual retreat allows an individual to listen to God's voice and experience God's healing grace that helps with spiritual renewal. Spiritual retreats have many purposes with some of them including participation in spiritual activities without the usual distractions of daily life and allowing an inner relaxation that can foster conversion of heart and deepening faith.

Our modern life is so full of stimulation, distraction, noise, and stress, that often God, or at least the thought of God, is lost in the bombardment of other things. The Catholic Encyclopedia describes the need for retreats is this way: *In the fever and agitation of modern life, the need for meditation and spiritual repose impresses itself on Christian souls who desire to reflect on their eternal destiny and direct their life in this world towards God.*

Jesus knew long ago the need for spiritual retreats and confirms that this isn't just a modern situation. In the Gospel of Mark, Jesus taught us by example. *Very early in the morning, while it was still dark, Jesus got up, left the house and went off to a solitary place, where he prayed. Simon and his companions went to look for him, and when they found him, they exclaimed, "Everyone is looking for you!" (Mark 1:35-37)* Despite all the things he had to do, he knew that a time of prayer in a quiet place was needed to refresh and strengthened his soul. In fact, it is in prayer that we gain the strength to often do what it is that needs to be done. It is not only physical strength that we need but often even more so we need emotional and spiritual strength to meet the needs of the tasks at hand.

After working hard and fulfilling the duties of life we often need to go away to discern the deeper messages that are often hidden in our work, our encounters, and our accomplishments. Jesus teaches us just that through his actions with his apostles in Mark 6:30-32, *The apostles gathered together with Jesus and reported all that they had done and taught. He said to them, "Come away by yourselves to a deserted place and rest awhile." People were coming and going in great numbers, and they had no opportunity even to eat. So, they went off in the boat by themselves to a deserted place.*

Retreats can be as simple as a one-day getaway that allows for prayer, contemplation, discernment, and relaxation. Or they can be more structured like participating in a pilgrimage traveling to holy places like Assisi, the home of Saint Francis in Italy, or walking the Camino de Santigo, the 500-mile journey across northern Spain ending where Saint James is laid to rest. The types of retreats can be tailored to our needs, our time availability, and even our financial situation. Often the type of retreat isn't as important as the quality of the retreat and having the ability to disconnect for our routine and busy life and to connect prayerfully with God.

EXERCISE – What type of retreat would you like to make? List two types:

1. _____
2. _____

Let us pray,

Oh Lord,
You know my heart better than I know it myself.
You know my struggles and You hold each hope and fear in Your caring hands.
Teach me, LORD, to be still and to know that You are God.
Amen.

Day 64

Be Not Afraid

Are you aware that the words *Be Not Afraid* are listed in the Bible 365 times? That is as many as one per day of the year. Is that a coincidence? The devil uses fear to often keep us from fully embracing our Christian lives. He knows that if we have a sense that we might not succeed, or if we could be persecuted even in the smallest of ways, or just being fearful that things will not turn out the way we have imagined, that we might not proceed with something that could be truly transformational and good. This sense of fear has paralyzed so many in the world.

What is it in life that will help us to overcome fear? It is faith and trust. As we conform our life to be a life of prayer and service to our Lord, our faith will grow as our relationship grows with Christ. The more intimate we become with Christ the more we begin to understand who He is and who we are too. It is in this relationship that we begin to understand on a much deeper level God's unique plan and vision for us and how we are called to serve out that plan during the short time that we are here on earth. In that plan, there will be times of success and even times of difficulty. Yet, all of it, the good, the bad, and even the ugly, is all a part of that plan and God will ensure that we are cared for along the way.

One of the greatest popes of all time was Saint John Paul II. When he became pope and addressed the world, included in his first speech were the words *Be Not Afraid.* He recognized that in our world so many had become fearful and that Christ's light and His message were being stifled. He shared, *"So often today man does not know what is within him, in the depths of his mind and heart. So often he is uncertain about the meaning of his life on this earth. He is assailed by doubt, a doubt which turns into despair. We ask you therefore, we beg you with humility and trust, let Christ speak to man. He alone has words of life, yes, of eternal life."* He further proclaimed, *"Brothers and sisters, do not be afraid to welcome Christ and accept his power. Help the Pope and all those who wish to serve Christ and with Christ's power to serve the human person and the whole of mankind. Do not be afraid. Open wide the doors for Christ."*

How is it that we are to open wide the doors for Christ? In Matthew 6:25-34, Christ tells us:

- "Therefore, I tell you, do not be anxious about your life, what you shall eat or what you shall drink, nor about your body, what you shall put on. Is not life more than food, and the body more than clothing? Look at the birds of the air: they neither sow nor reap nor gather into barns, and yet your heavenly Father feeds them. Are you not of more value than they? And which of you by being anxious can add one cubit to his span of life? And why are you anxious about clothing?

- Consider the lilies of the field, how they grow; they neither toil nor spin; yet I tell you, even Solomon in all his glory was not arrayed like one of these. But if God so clothes the grass of the field, which today is alive and tomorrow is thrown into the oven, will he not much more clothe you, O men of little faith? Therefore, do not be anxious, saying, 'What shall we eat?' or 'What shall we drink?' or 'What shall we wear?' For the Gentiles seek all these things, and your heavenly Father knows that you need them all. But seek first his kingdom and his righteousness, and all these things shall be yours as well.

- "Therefore, do not be anxious about tomorrow, for tomorrow will be anxious for itself. Let the day's own trouble be sufficient for the day."

Let us today pray for God to work within our hearts to help us to build trust and to open wide the doors of Christ,

Lord,
give me a fervent heart of prayer.
Help me to be open to those whom You place in my path.
And as I pray for those in need,
I make myself available to You to be used as You will.
Jesus, I trust in You.
Amen.

100 days to Freedom

Day 65

Fifth Commandment - You Shall Not Kill

So many Christians give little thought to the Fifth Commandment thinking that if they don't murder another person then they are good and can wipe the Fifth Commandment off their list of things to be worried or concerned about. Yet, they are missing the greater details in the guide to freedom that the commandment was meant to be. One can kill in many ways in addition to murder. The following list that is intended to be a self-reflection during an examination of conscience will be helpful to allow us to see more deeply into God's directive.

EXERCISE – Please answer the following questions.

Have I…

- Unjustly and intentionally killed a human being?
- Been involved in an abortion, directly or indirectly (through advice, etc.)?
- Seriously considered or attempted suicide?
- Supported, promoted, or encouraged the practice of assisted suicide or mercy killing?
- Deliberately desired to kill an innocent human being?
- Unjustly inflicted bodily harm upon another person?
- Unjustly threatened another person with bodily harm?
- Verbally or emotionally abused another person?
- Hated another person, or wished him evil?
- Been prejudiced, or unjustly discriminated against others because of their race, color, nationality, sex or religion?
- Joined a hate group?
- Purposely provoked another by teasing or nagging?
- Recklessly endangered my life or health, or that of another, by my actions?
- Driven recklessly or under the influence of alcohol or other drugs?

- Abused alcohol or other drugs?
- Sold or given drugs to others to use for non-therapeutic purposes?
- Used tobacco immoderately?
- Over-eaten?
- Encouraged others to sin by giving scandal?
- Helped another to commit a mortal sin (through advice, driving them somewhere, etc.?)
- Caused serious injury or death by criminal neglect?
- Indulged in serious anger?
- Refused to control my temper?
- Been mean to, quarreled with, or willfully hurt someone?
- Been unforgiving to others, when mercy or pardon was requested?
- Sought revenge or hoped something bad would happen to someone?
- Delighted to see someone else get hurt or suffer?
- Treated animals cruelly, causing them to suffer or die needlessly?

Although not all the items contained in the above questions would be so egregious to warrant the classification of mortal sin, a complete separation from God, they do help us to understand that through related actions there is much more to the commandment. At a minimum, answering 'yes' to any of the questions, specifically the lesser in severity, would be considered sinful actions, venial sins, and we would want to ask for forgiveness to remove their effects from our souls.

Let us pray,

Eternal God,
You have revealed Yourself as the Father of all Life.
We praise You for the Fatherly care which You extend to all creation,
and especially to us, made in Your image and likeness.
Father, extend Your hand of protection to those threatened by abortion,
and save them from its destructive power.
Give Your strength to all fathers, that they may never give in to the fears
that may tempt them to facilitate abortions.
Bless our families and bless our land, that we may have the joy of
welcoming and nurturing the life of which You are the source and the Eternal Father.
Amen.

Day 66

Trusting in God's Providence

So often we find ourselves consumed with fear and anxiety. Often, we have no idea as to why we are filled with so much negative energy. It might be related to decisions we have to make or the choices we are making in life. It might be related to a feeling of possibly letting someone down even when our actions are not destructive in nature.

It was once said that most of the anxiety that people experience in life has to do with fear. Some of those fears are as follows:

1. The fear of inadequacy
2. The fear of uncertainty
3. The fear of failure
4. The fear of rejection
5. The fear of missing out
6. The fear of change
7. The fear of losing control
8. The fear of being judged
9. The fear of something bad happening
10. The fear of getting hurt

EXERCISE – Take a minute and reflect on the above list of fears and think about when you experience anxiety in your life, do any of these fears play a possible role in your reaction?

The Bible is filled with Scripture that describes God's providence. A few of those Scripture verses are as follows:

- *And my God will supply every need of yours according to His riches in glory in Christ Jesus.*
- *Look at the birds of the air: they neither sow nor reap nor gather into barns, and yet your heavenly Father feeds them. Are you not of more value than they?*
- *Do not be anxious about anything, but in everything by prayer and supplication with thanksgiving let your requests be made known to God.*
- *If you then, who are evil, know how to give good gifts to your children, how much more will your Father who is in heaven give good things to those who ask Him!*
- *If we are faithless, He remains faithful—for He cannot deny himself.*

When we experience fear and anxiety in our lives it is often due to forgetting that God is in command, and that He knows exactly what we need and when we need it. He knows what will help us grow in virtue and what will lead us astray. He either wills things to happen, or allows things to happen but always to help us along our journey towards deeper intimacy with Him. The more we can place our trust in our Lord and our God, the less we will experience anxiety and fear in our lives. Once we understand that as long as we are serving Him to the best of our ability, living in the truth, and attempting to follow the way established by Christ Himself, we will be cared for in the manner that we need to be cared for. This is trust. This is faith. We are disciples that believe and have faith. We only need to be reminded of this from time-to-time.

Let us pray,

O my God,
I firmly believe that Thou art one God,
in three Divine Persons,
the Father, the Son and the Holy Ghost;
I believe that Thy Divine Son became man and died for our sins
and that He will come to judge the living and the dead.
I believe these and all the truths which the holy Catholic Church teaches,
because Thou hast revealed them, Who canst neither deceive nor be deceived.
Amen.

100 days to Freedom

Day 67

The Rosary (From Dynamic Catholic)

The Rosary is such a powerful spiritual tool but still today so many either don't understand its significance or have misguided thoughts about it. Why do so many pray the Rosary? Quite simply, the Rosary works. Here are 10 reasons why to pray the Rosary?

1. Peace. We live hectic lives in a chaotic world. All this can lead to a confusion that fogs the mind, unsettles the soul, and leads to poor decisions. Amidst all this chaos and confusion our souls yearn for peace and clarity. There is just something about the Rosary that settles our hearts and minds. It reaches deep down into our souls and puts us at ease, creating a peace that is rare and beautiful.

2. Perspective. Do you ever feel like stepping back from the world? Do you ever feel like taking a nice, long, extended break from the daily commitments and responsibilities? The Rosary is a great way to do that. It allows us to leave the world behind for a little while and get some perspective. By praying the Rosary, we get to step back from who we are, where we are, and what we're doing, and reassess who we are and what on earth we are doing.

3. Always What We Need. The Rosary is ever fresh, ever new, and deeply personal. Every time we pray it, we can have a completely different experience than we did yesterday or last week. Of course, the Rosary doesn't change, but we do. Our questions change. Our struggles and concerns change. Our faith and doubts change. Where we are in our journey with God changes. The Rosary provides the context, the format, and the process for God to speak to us about all these things.

4. Mary. Nobody sees the life of a child the way that child's mother does—not even the father. This is Mary's perspective of Jesus' life. She has a unique perspective. It seems that every genuine Christian, not just Catholics, should be interested in that perspective—and not just interested, but fascinated. In the
Rosary we ponder the life of Jesus through the eyes of his mother. This is an incredibly powerful experience if we enter into it fully.

5. Awareness. This is a giant benefit from praying the Rosary, and it is central to a rich and vibrant spiritual life. Being aware of what is happening inside, around us, and to us, is one of the most incredible gifts God can give us. One of the rarest gifts that awareness freely gives us is the ability to see things as they really are. This extraordinary clarity tends to make those who possess it very good decision-makers. The many ways we can pray and reflect with the Rosary help us grow in awareness.

6. Epic Moments. When we pray the Rosary, we reflect on some of the most epic moments in history. For example, the Annunciation, Mary's moment, the moment when her "yes" changed the world. Imagine the monumental courage that would have required. Think about it. Everything hung in the balance. What would have happened if Mary had said no? And there are 20 of these moments in the different mysteries of the Rosary. Imagine what we can learn.

7. Slow Down. Praying the Rosary regularly encourages us to slow down, which in turn should encourage us to live life at a different pace than the rest of the world. We learn from Mary how to look at an experience, hold it in our hearts, and ponder what it means for our lives. This slower pace also allows us to be present. The Rosary will teach you to be 100% present to whoever and whatever is in front of you at any given moment.

8. Community. When we come together, great things can happen. When we come together to pray the Rosary, even greater things can happen. The Rosary has the power to impact the lives of our loved ones, our communities, and our nation. What can we pray for? We can pray for the needs of our families and friends. We can pray for our communities, for our cities and neighborhoods, for our schools and churches, and for the hungry, lonely, and sick. We can pray for our nation, our leaders, and our troops. Praying the Rosary can bring peace to a troubled world, healing to broken hearts, and clarity to those in chaos.

9. The-Best-Version-of-Ourselves. Praying the Rosary helps us look at who we are and challenges us to become a-better-version-of-ourselves. We become intimately familiar with the better person we know we can be—a better friend, a better parent, a better spouse, a better child and sibling, a better employer and leader, a better citizen of this country, and a better member of the human family.

10. Healing. Who doesn't need their history healed? Who doesn't want to be rescued from the turbulence and anxiety of modern life? Who doesn't want their soul healed? Every time you pray the Rosary, Jesus welcomes you into his life and you welcome him into your life. Bring him your deepest pains and struggles and let him heal the hurt. Only great things can happen when you invite Jesus into your life.

Day 68

Littleness

Often people misunderstand the concept of littleness. They initially think of it as being weak or incapable. Yet, in the spiritual life, littleness means something much different. Littleness falls in line with humility. It is the understanding of who and what we are in relation to God. When we think of God as the Creator, the "I AM" that nothing can be compared to, how else can we see ourselves but as littleness.

Being little means that we understand that all things that are accomplished are so because God has willed it. It does not mean that we should not have goals and should stop striving towards grand things, but that we are to have the understanding that when we do come upon success it is God that we are to thank. God is the one who has bestowed upon us any talent that we might possess. God is the one who has allowed things to fall into place so that our goals and plans can come to fruition.

In our littleness is how we become strong. Realizing that God knows everything about us, what we need, what is best for our continual spiritual development, and that He cares and loves us more than we can imagine. This should give reassurance that there is nothing in life that God has not directly willed or allowed to happen. We also know through Scripture that God will not give us more than we can handle even though we might think otherwise from time to time.

No trial has come to you but what is human.
God is faithful and will not let you be tried beyond your strength;
but with the trial, he will also provide a way out, so that you may be able to bear it.
1 Cor 10:13

When we find the courage to overcome our sinful pride and surrender to God, is when we are strengthened in God's love and power. Our strength in God shines brightest in the light of our weakness. Yet, our weakness is also our strength.

EXERCISE – Take a moment and think about a few times in your life when you felt weak or little and then about how maybe God was working within you at the same time.

Experience of weakness or littleness	How God used that situation to allow growth?

Let us pray,

O Jesus! meek and humble of heart, Hear me.
From the desire of being esteemed, Deliver me, Jesus.
From the desire of being loved, Deliver me, Jesus.
From the desire of being extolled, Deliver me, Jesus.
From the desire of being honored, Deliver me, Jesus.
From the desire of being praised, Deliver me, Jesus.
From the desire of being preferred to others, Deliver me, Jesus.
From the desire of being consulted, Deliver me, Jesus.
From the desire of being approved, Deliver me, Jesus.
From the fear of being humiliated, Deliver me, Jesus.
From the fear of being despised, Deliver me, Jesus.
From the fear of suffering rebukes, Deliver me, Jesus.
From the fear of being calumniated, Deliver me, Jesus.
From the fear of being forgotten, Deliver me, Jesus.
From the fear of being ridiculed, Deliver me, Jesus.
From the fear of being wronged, Deliver me, Jesus.
From the fear of being suspected, Deliver me, Jesus.
That others may be loved more than I. Amen.

Day 69

Mercy and Forgiveness

One of our greatest weaknesses is our ability to hold onto resentment and anger. Yet, how many of us would want just the opposite from God, to forgive us for our past trespasses and provide mercy? Of all the prayers, the *Our Father,* the prayer that Jesus taught to us when He was asked by his disciples how is it that we are to pray, would be considered our most holy prayer. Within that holy and special prayer are the words, "…Forgive us our trespasses as we forgive those who trespass against us…"

The word mercy comes from the Latin word *misericordia*, derived from the two words *miserere* ("pity" or "misery") and *cor* ("heart"). So, when we are asking for mercy, we are essentially asking God to free us from a heart that is in misery. Our hearts are in a state of misery due to the sinfulness of our lives and it is the sin that is creating so much pain. However, it doesn't always have to be because of sin that we are experiencing so much hurt. It can be from a variety of things such as broken relationships, the loss of a job, physical and mental health issues, being betrayed, and even spiritual and physical poverty.

There are other ways to think about mercy and looking to the seven-spiritual works of mercy will shed some additional insight.

1. **To instruct the ignorant.** This work of mercy means all of us are called to share and teach the faith passed on to us. This, of course, means that we must know our faith and what our Church really teaches. And the best way to instruct and to teach is by example.

2. **To counsel the doubtful.** Every one of us has doubts and questions about our faith. Even Saint Mother Teresa had dark nights of the soul wherein she felt doubt and despair. This work of mercy reminds us how important it is to walk closely with people going through transitions, loss or great trials, holding them up in prayer and companionship.

3. **To admonish the sinner**. This one is very hard to do, especially if one is honest about his/her own life. "People in glass houses should not throw stones. But, nonetheless, this third work of mercy calls us to dialog with others about any sinful behavior that may exist. Here is where love and charity need to be used with words chosen carefully so that one doesn't come off preachy, nagging or "holier than thou". This one is not easy.

4. **To bear wrongs patiently.** Here our pride is the culprit and revenge the temptation. The words of Jesus, "Turn the other cheek" ring out, but that is not easy to do. And I think it is sometimes harder to endure wrongs and to be patient with hardship when someone is doing harm to our children or grandchildren.

5. **To forgive offenses willingly.** This work of mercy is inseparably bound with the patient endurance of wrongdoing. Forgiveness takes time, and even though one does not feel completely at peace with the other, the desire to want to forgive is the beginning of the road to full forgiveness. What helps me to forgive another is the promise from the Lord Jesus, "As many times as you forgive others, that's how many times I'll forgive you."

6. **To comfort the afflicted.** There are times when we see someone going through a bad time and we can't take it away from him or from her. Our words are inadequate and our actions pointless. All we can do is walk silently with him or her in love and prayer.

7. **To pray for the living and the dead**. Clearly the most important part of any work of mercy, be it spiritual or corporal is prayer. Prayer that seeks to unite us to God changes the physical act of feeding the poor into a spiritual act that does good to another and gives God the glory. As one writer says, "Our private intercession for our neighbors and for the departed brings us little fame or admiration from others, but in the end, when we stand before God, we will be able to give an account of our prayerful mercy to others, and so Jesus will, in turn, show us mercy."

Let us pray,

Lord,
Have mercy on me and the whole world.
Amen.

Day 70

Congratulations, you have made it to day 70. This is a good time to stop, take a deep breath, and to evaluate how well, or maybe how not so well, the disciplines are going. Please take a minute, break out a pen or pencil, and complete this very important self-evaluation regarding adherence.

Spiritual	1 No Action	2 Almost none	3 Hit and miss	4 Almost perfect	5 Nailed it!
Daily Mass or Daily Mass readings and Spiritual Communion					
Daily Rosary					
Formal Examination of Conscience nightly					
Daily Spiritual reading					
Weekly adoration in front of the Blessed Sacrament					
Monthly Confession					

Physical	1 No Action	2 Almost none	3 Hit and miss	4 Almost perfect	5 Nailed it!
Walk or Run daily					
Push-ups / Sit-ups / Lunges daily or weight lifting					
Stretches daily					
7-8 hours' sleep a night					

Nutrition	1 No Action	2 Almost none	3 Hit and miss	4 Almost perfect	5 Nailed it!
2-3 meals a day - No eating between meals					
No candy / desserts					
No fast-food					
Fasting on Mon / Wed / Friday					

Self-Denial	1 No Action	2 Almost none	3 Hit and miss	4 Almost perfect	5 Nailed it!
No major purchases (Toiletries and needed items only)					
No TV or movies					
No social media					
No Alcohol					

Well, how did you do? Let me guess, maybe less than perfect? Join the club, I have yet to meet the perfect human or the one who completed the entire *100 days to Freedom* program without missing a discipline even once. That makes you normal, human, and maybe a little less than a superhero. Yet, as Christians, we are called toward a path of perfection, a life of holiness, a life in which we journey closer and closer to God.

The structure of this program will allow each of us to grow, to grow in virtue, character, self-discipline, and in relationship with God. Reflect once again on the scores you gave yourself above and then on the categories: Spiritual Life, Physical Health, Nutritional Health, and Self-Discipline. If you identify an area where there is more opportunity for growth, then try to place a greater focus on that area for the next week.

We have all been created in God's image and likeness, and we have been created as unique individuals. No two journeys are alike, just like no two scorecards are exactly alike. God is working in us in the exact way He feels that He needs to work in us to help us to travel our unique journey. Let go and allow Him to drive this journey. Our part is to be open to His promptings and respond when He calls.

Keep up the good work and as you progress day-by-day be prepared to enjoy the rewards that God has ready for you. Whenever we turn our focus away from ourselves and upon the Lord, we begin to realize what freedom truly feels and looks like.

Let us pray,

Father, look upon our weakness and reach out to help us with Your loving power.
You redeem us and make us Your children in Christ.
Look upon us, give us true freedom and bring us to the inheritance You promised.
We ask this through our Lord Jesus Christ, Your Son,
who lives and reigns with You and the Holy Spirit,
one God, forever and ever. Amen.

Day 71

The Sixth Commandment – You shall not commit adultery

The sexes are meant by divine design to be different and complementary, each having equal dignity and made in the image of God. Sexual acts are sacred within the context of the marital relationship that reflects a "complete and lifelong mutual gift of a man and a woman." Sexual sins thus violate not just the body, but the person's whole being.

Sex is more than a physical act, it also affects one's body and soul. Related to the issue of sex, there is the issue of chastity which is a virtue that all people are called to acquire. Chastity is defined as the inner unity of a person's "bodily and spiritual being" that successfully integrates a person's sexuality with his or her "entire human nature." To acquire this virtue, followers are encouraged to enter into the "long and exacting work" of self-mastery that is helped by friendships, God's grace, maturity and education "that respects the moral and spiritual dimensions of human life." The Catechism categorizes violations of the Sixth Commandment into two categories: "offenses against chastity" and "offenses against the dignity of marriage."

Offenses Against Chastity

Lust: The Church teaches that sexual pleasure is good and created by God, who meant for spouses to "experience pleasure and enjoyment of body and spirit". Lust is the desire for sexual pleasure alone, outside its intended purpose of procreation and the uniting of man and woman, body and soul, in mutual self-donation. Masturbation is considered sinful for the same reasons as lust but is a step above lust in that it involves a physical act instead of a mental one.

Fornication is the sexual union of an unmarried man and an unmarried woman. This is considered contrary to "the dignity of persons and of human sexuality" because it is not ordered to the "good of spouses" or the "generation and education of children."

Pornography ranks higher because it is considered a perversion of the sexual act that is intended for distribution to third parties for viewing.

Prostitution is considered sinful for both the prostitute and the customer; it reduces a person to an instrument of sexual pleasure, violating human dignity and harming society. The gravity of the sinfulness is less for prostitutes who are forced into the act by destitution, blackmail or social pressure.

Rape is an intrinsically evil act that can cause grave damage to the victim for life. Incest, or "rape of children by parents or other adult relatives" or "those responsible for the education of the children entrusted to them" is considered the most heinous of sexual sins.

Love of Husband and Wife

Spousal love is intended to form an unbroken, two-fold end: the union of husband and wife and the transmission of life. The unitive aspect includes the transference of each partner's being "so that they are no longer two but one flesh." The sacrament of matrimony is viewed as God's sealing the consent which binds the partners together. Church teaching on the marital state requires spousal acceptance of each other's failures and faults, and the recognition that the "call to holiness in marriage" is one that requires a process of spiritual growth and conversion that can last throughout life.

The Church position on sexual activity can be summarized as: "sexual activity belongs only in marriage as an expression of total self-giving and union, and always open to the possibility of new life." Sexual acts in marriage are considered "noble and honorable" and are meant to be enjoyed with "joy and gratitude." Sexuality is to be reserved to marriage: by its very nature conjugal love requires the inviolable fidelity of the spouses. This is the consequence of the gift of themselves which they make to each other.

Homosexuality

Basing itself on Sacred Scripture, which presents homosexual acts as acts of grave depravity, tradition has always declared that "homosexual acts are intrinsically disordered." They are contrary to the natural law. They close the sexual act to the gift of life. They do not proceed from a genuine affective and sexual complementarity. Under no circumstances can they be approved. The number of men and women who have deep-seated homosexual tendencies is not negligible. This inclination, which is objectively disordered, constitutes for most of them a trial. They must be accepted with respect, compassion, and sensitivity. These persons are called to fulfill God's will in their lives and, if they are Christians, to unite to the sacrifice of the Lord's Cross the difficulties they may encounter from their condition.

Day 72

Walking

Walking has become almost nonexistent in our modern culture. We drive cars and motorcycles, we take buses and taxis everywhere and by doing so we are missing out on the numerous effects of walking. Yes, there are health benefits of walking, but there is much more than that. When we walk, time slows down, and we can experience the things around us in a much deeper way. We can take in the smells around us. We can feel the temperature. Our feet can feel the pavement or the rocks. We communicate with those along our path and can sense the moods of people. As we walk near others, we can visualize how they are walking, their posture, their pace. We can hear animals and even church bells ringing in the distance. Our senses are livened, and as previously mentioned time slows down, and our minds absorb even the smallest of details as we walk.

In contrast to walking, when we travel in cars although we think we are saving time, we are in reality losing time. What is meant by this statement, is that as we travel with great speed our minds are not able to take in the sensations around us and by the time we arrive at our destination nothing has been registered in our minds about the travel experience. At least the details of what could have been experienced by walking will not be there.

When we walk, we are also given the opportunity to ponder ideas. As the rush of distractions are cleared away from our lives during the walking process, we can explore our thoughts and ideas and allow our imaginations to soar with potential. Many have said that their best ideas and their level of creativity are at their highest during their periods of walking.

For many, their time of walking has also become their time of prayer. Some who have difficulty sitting still to pray, find no difficulty speaking and listening to God as they walk. A walk, especially a Godly walk in nature can be spiritually healing and nourishing.

There are differences with brief walks and walks of longer duration. Having routine walks lasting for three to five hours can do wonders for the mind and the soul. These prolonged walks allow for the body to release a variety of neurochemicals in the bloodstream and body and by doing so can act as antidepressants. It was once said that if a person is in a bad mood then they should go for a walk. If they return from their walk and are still in a bad mood, then they should go for another walk. The statement can be taken humorously, but there is also truth in it as well. Long walks clear the mind, can give an opportunity to ponder life-events, to rationalize solutions, free the body of stress, and flood the body with healing chemicals.

CHALLENGE – Plan how you will incorporate more walking into your life and how you will plan for a routine of long walks.

Let us pray,

Lord Jesus Christ, I come in need to walk in the hope that only You can give.

My way is unclear. The path is sometimes filled with twists and turns and confusion.

Show me Your ways, Lord. Show me how You would walk in these places.

Teach me Your paths of grace, mercy, integrity, and love. Help me to grasp Your ways so I can walk securely in them, even in the valley of darkness.

Lord, I need to know Your perspective. Help me, Lord Jesus, to focus on Your ways.

Amen.

Use this section below to journal any thoughts or inspirations from the meditation to help with further reflection.

_____

_____

_____

_____

_____

_____

_____

100 days to Freedom

Day 73

Charism

What is a charism?

Charisms, spiritual gifts, are special abilities, a special empowerment, given to a Christian by the Holy Spirit to enable them to be powerful channels of God's love and redeeming presence in the World. Whether extraordinary or ordinary, charisms are to be used in charity or service to build up the Church (CATECHISM OF THE CATHOLIC CHURCH, 2003).

A charism is always deeply connected with our faith and is an expression of our relationship with God. In this way, it differs from a natural or learned ability. A charism, exercised correctly, draws other people to God. For instance, we can take art courses and learn to paint a picture. The ceiling of the Sistine Chapel, however, draws people to God. Stained glass windows in a church do the same.

We have all been gifted with a special and often unique charism that makes us who we are and allows us to fulfill our mission here on earth. At the core of this mission is to serve God and his people while at the same time growing towards union with God. These charisms are special to each of us in the sense that they are gifts or abilities that will help us in our missionary lives. Some examples of charisms or spiritual gifts are as follows:

Prophet: In the New Testament, the office of prophet is to equip the saints for the work of service through exhortation, edification, and consolation (1 Corinthians 12:28; 1 Corinthians 14:3 Ephesians 4:11). The prophet's corresponding gift is prophecy. Prophecy is "reporting something that God spontaneously brings to your mind."

Evangelist: An evangelist is one who devotes himself to preaching the gospel. In the New Testament, evangelists preached from city to city, church to church.

Teacher: Someone who devotes his or her life to preaching and teaching the Christian faith. When teaching is provided for the Church by God, two gifts are actually given - to the Church is given a teacher and along with the teacher comes a divine capacity to teach.

Service: The word translated as "ministry" is Diakonia, which can also be translated "service." Since there are many types of ministries and service to the Church, this then describes a broad array of gifts rather than a single gift.

Exhortation: The ability to motivate Christians "to patient endurance, brotherly love, and good works."

Giving: Those with this gift share their own possessions with others with extraordinary generosity. While all Christians should be givers, those possessing this gift will go beyond this normal giving.

Leading: This gift speaks to the various leadership roles found in the Church.

Mercy: Possibly identical to the gift of helps, the mercy-shower possesses a ministry of visitation, prayer, and compassion to the poor and sick.

Faith: This refers to that strong or special faith "which removes mountains, casts out devils (Matthew 17:19–20), and faces the cruelest martyrdom without flinching."

Healing: The ability to supernaturally minister healing to others.

Helps: This gift has to do with service to the sick and the poor. Possessor of this gift has a "spiritual burden and a God-given love for the needy and afflicted."

EXERCISE: What do you think your charism might be? _____

How do you use this? _____

Day 74

Cardinal Virtues (From the Catechism of the Catholic Church)

A virtue is a habitual and firm disposition to do the good. It allows the person not only to perform good acts, but to give the best of himself. The virtuous person tends toward the good with all his sensory and spiritual powers; he pursues the good and chooses it in concrete actions. The goal of a virtuous life is to become like God.

Human virtues are firm attitudes, stable dispositions, habitual perfections of intellect and will that govern our actions, order our passions, and guide our conduct according to reason and faith. They make possible ease self-mastery and joy in leading a morally good life. The virtuous man is he who freely practices the good.

The moral virtues are acquired by human effort. They are the fruit and seed of morally good acts; they dispose all the powers of the human being for communion with divine love.

Four virtues play a pivotal role and accordingly are called "cardinal"; all the others are grouped around them. They are **prudence, justice, fortitude, and temperance.** "If anyone loves righteousness, [Wisdom's] labors are virtues; for she teaches temperance and prudence, justice, and courage." These virtues are praised under other names in many passages of Scripture.

Prudence is the virtue that disposes practical reason to discern our true good in every circumstance and to choose the right means of achieving it; "the prudent man looks where he is going." "Keep sane and sober for your prayers." Prudence is "right reason in action," writes St. Thomas Aquinas, following Aristotle. It is not to be confused with timidity or fear, nor with duplicity or dissimulation. It is called Auriga Virtutum (the charioteer of the virtues); it guides the other virtues by setting rule and measure. It is prudence that immediately guides the judgment of conscience.

The prudent man determines and directs his conduct in accordance with this judgment. With the help of this virtue we apply moral principles to particular cases without error and overcome doubts about the good to achieve and the evil to avoid.

Justice is the moral virtue that consists in the constant and firm will to give their due to God and neighbor. Justice toward God is called the "virtue of religion." Justice toward men disposes one to respect the rights of each and to establish in human relationships the harmony that promotes equity with regard to persons and to the common good. The just man, often mentioned in the Sacred Scripture, is distinguished by habitual right thinking and the uprightness of his conduct toward his neighbor. "You shall not be partial to the poor or defer to the great, but in righteousness shall you judge your neighbor." "Masters, treat your slaves justly and fairly, knowing that you also have a Master in heaven."

Fortitude is the moral virtue that ensures firmness in difficulties and constancy in the pursuit of the good. It strengthens the resolve to resist temptations and to overcome obstacles in the moral life. The virtue of fortitude enables one to conquer fear, even fear of death, and to face trials and persecutions. It disposes one even to renounce and sacrifice his life in defense of a just cause. "The Lord is my strength and my song." "In the world you have tribulation; but be of good cheer, I have overcome the world."

Temperance is the moral virtue that moderates the attraction of pleasures and provides balance in the use of created goods. It ensures the will's mastery over instincts and keeps desires within the limits of what is honorable. The temperate person directs the sensitive appetites toward what is good and maintains a healthy discretion: "Do not follow your inclination and strength, walking according to the desires of your heart." Temperance is often praised in the Old Testament: "Do not follow your base desires but restrain your appetites." In the New Testament it is called "moderation" or "sobriety." We ought "to live sober, upright, and godly lives in this world."

To live well is nothing other than to love God with all one's heart, with all one's soul, and with all one's efforts; from this it comes about that love is kept whole and uncorrupted (through temperance). No misfortune can disturb it (and this is fortitude). It obeys only [God] (and this is justice), and is careful in discerning things, so as not to be surprised by deceit or trickery (and this is prudence).

Let us pray,

Jesus, I trust in you. Jesus, I trust in you. Jesus, I trust in you.
Amen.

100 days to Freedom

Day 75

Holy Marriage

Scripture tells us that it is not good for man to be alone and that God wanted to make a suitable partner for him. God initially created animals to be man's companions, but none proved to be a suitable partner. So, God created woman. But He didn't just create a woman out of nothing as he could have; He took a piece of the man and created her. The man replied to the creation "This one, at last, is bone of my bones and flesh of my flesh." Jesus teaches us that they are no longer two but one flesh and speaking of the Sacrament of Marriage, "What God has joined together, no human being must separate."

We all know that over 50% of marriages end in divorce and that most of these were probably thought of as more of a "Contractual Marriage" (an agreement) than a Sacrament. A Sacramental Marriage is a covenant by which a man a woman establishes between themselves a partnership for the whole of life. Usually, we think of this covenant in a rather personal and individual context. It exists for the good of the spouses and the good of their children. We sometimes think of the wedding ceremony, which establishes this covenant as belonging to the Bride and Groom, as if it were their wedding alone. They can invite whomever they want, sing their favorite songs, and arrange the ceremony as they please. However, the Second Vatican Council reminds us that the Marriage covenant exists not only for the good of the partners and their children but also for the good of the Church and the good of society at large. Marriage is a Sacrament.

In each of the Sacraments, a window opens, and we can glimpse the mystery of God and God's plan for the salvation of the world. In a Christian Marriage, we see that God was not content to be alone. Out of love, God created us and all that is. God is faithful no matter what. Whether we are faithful or faithless, God is faithful; whether we wander away in sin or remain in the embrace of love, God is always there and is ever ready to embrace us. This Sacramental Sign, which the husband and wife give to each other, they also give to the entire community of witnesses. Although most of us have never personally seen God, the Sacramental Marriage and the love and relationship that flows between a husband and wife is one of the closest things we have on this earth that represents God's relationship with us. The fidelity of Christian husbands and wives represents that love and that relationship that God offers to us. This relationship is a mystery, a mystery for sure.

We live in a culture that in many ways has forgotten the holiness and permanence of marriage. Almost all of us have had some connection with a divorce. Divorce always brings hurt, pain, and can leave scars that last a lifetime, if not for the spouses, almost always for the children. We as Christians should understand that God does not desire for us to be alone. He desires communion between us, with Jesus, and ultimately with Him. There is no greater want in this world than the desire to be loved. However, to be loved, one must love. To be forgiven, one must forgive, to be understood, one must understand. God has given us much more than we could ever give in return. This understanding of God has been given to us as a guide for earthly living and earthly marriage and we should be eternally grateful. Of all the great obstacles in marriage today, not unlike the obstacles identified in history, these struggles usually have at their roots a common theme of pride or entitlement.

Pride and entitlement only create division and hurt. Yet one cannot feel grateful and entitled at the same time. If we could only view life and our relationships through grateful eyes, pride and entitlement would never be our burden. Gratitude and entitlement cannot share the same breath, nor thought. Think about this for a minute. Gratitude and entitlement are opposites; they cannot share the same breath, nor thought.

Marriage is a journey, where two individuals through God's grace, travel together, assist each other while growing in holiness, help pick each other up, support each other, forgive each other, love each other, and serve each other in the same manner as God does for us. That is what a Christian marriage is. That is what a sacramental marriage is.

Trials, temptations, and obstacles are a part of every marriage. Yet, if we focus our attention on God, seek our God for answers, strengthened by the Sacraments, and can transcend our own self-will, imitate God's love, mercy, and permanence, our marriages will be fruitful beyond belief. Our Sacramental marriages will be fruitful beyond belief!

Day 76

Community

God did not create us to live in isolation. He created us to live amongst each other and to benefit from each other. This benefit comes in a variety of ways. Being connected and involved with a community helps us to see the world with a much broader lens. We can become teachers and students of each other as we interact and spend time together.

1. Community challenges you to be more like Jesus. (HEBREWS 10:24-25) Nothing makes you more like Jesus than the daily grind of interactions with others. We often think about marriage when it comes to this refining process, but the truth is God also gives us community as a way to become more like Him. God's Word reminds us that we are put in relationships in order to encourage one another in our pursuit of God and His Kingdom. It's within the context of community that we are given the opportunity to be refined as followers of Christ.

2. Community meets practical needs. (ACTS 2:42-47) Just like in the early Church, community is a place where we come to get our physical needs met. We need to learn to let down our walls and ask for help from our brothers and sisters in Christ. Whether we need someone to pick up medicine for us when we're sick, cook us a meal at the end of a long week or help us carry a financial burden, the Body of Christ was made to support and love one another in practical ways. We can learn a lot about love within the exchange of practical needs.

3. Community carries you emotionally. (GALATIANS 6:2) The emotional needs that we carry through life are just as important as our physical needs. We are given the responsibility to support each other in hard times and to carry one another's burdens. As much as we need to be available for our brothers and sisters in Christ, we also need to have the courage to ask them to come alongside us when we're the ones in need of support, prayer, or a shoulder to cry on. It's important to learn to be real with one another because that's what true community is all about.

4. Community reveals your gifts and talents. (ECCLESIASTES 4:9-12) Two are better than one, because there is double the strength, double the stamina, and double the talents. Within the context of community, we're given the opportunity to discover our gifts and our talents and then use them to bless others. We're each given a very specific role in the Body of Christ, and it is within these relationships that our roles can be used to glorify God to the fullest. We're part of something really special (1 Corinthians 12:27).

5. Community opens your eyes to the needs of others. (1 THESSALONIANS 5:14) Within community, we are encouraged to look around at the needs of those around us. We're called to strengthen those who are weak and to and encourage those who are down and out. Community calls us out of our self-centeredness and self-absorption by giving us the responsibility to look outward.

6. Community empowers your relationship with God. (PROVERBS 27:17) There is something real about the concept of power in numbers. When we are surrounded by other believers, we feel empowered in our faith and may even be more sensitive to God's presence in our lives. There's something powerful about believers joining together, making each other accountable and being a sort of a witness of one another's lives. We need people checking in on us, asking the hard questions, and challenging us to really live out our faith.

7. Community helps meet our need for love. (PROVERBS 17:17) There's no denying that we are men and women who crave love. We were made by a relational God who longs for us to be in relationship with Him. But even more amazing is that God gives us the gift of each other as a way to meet our earthly needs for love. This brotherly love (phileo) that we're given is a beautiful representation of the greatest Friend who laid down His life for us. We're also called to love each other in this beautiful way.

8. Community teaches you to work through conflicts. (1 CORINTHIANS 1:10) Bring any group of people together and one thing is certain: conflict is inevitable. But we're called to work through our divisions with one another as the body of believers. We're asked to be a united body, which isn't always easy or natural. It's a humbling experience that teaches us to lay down our pride, to learn assertiveness, and to enhance our communication. We need each other because it's within the messiness of relationships with one other that we're reminded of our desperate need for Him.

9. Community gives you the chance to forgive. (1 PETER 4:8-11) There is nothing more beautiful than the picture of the gospel displayed through our healthy interactions as a body of believers. Within this body, we're bound to get hurt, and then guaranteed the opportunity to forgive. We get to feel what Jesus felt as He suffered wounds at the hands of the people He loved and then loved them anyway. This is the hardest part about community, but it's the part that makes us most like Him. Every day we are called to become more like Jesus, and community is one of the ways that we are invited to do so. So, what does that look like in your life?

Day 77

Stay Awake

It can become very easy to fall asleep in the routine of our lives while going through the motions of work, play, and rest. This falling asleep refers to forgetting the precepts of being a Christian and living life in such a way that Jesus had taught and commanded us to live.

Gospel (Mathew 24:37-44)

Jesus said to his disciples:
"As it was in the days of Noah,
so it will be at the coming of the Son of Man.
In those days before the flood,
they were eating and drinking,
marrying and giving in marriage,
up to the day that Noah entered the ark.
They did not know until the flood came and carried them all away.
So will it be also at the coming of the Son of Man.
Two men will be out in the field;
one will be taken, and one will be left.
Two women will be grinding at the mill;
one will be taken, and one will be left.
Therefore, stay awake!
For you do not know on which day your Lord will come.
Be sure of this: if the master of the house
had known the hour of night when the thief was coming,
he would have stayed awake
and not let his house be broken into.
So too, you also must be prepared,
for at an hour you do not expect, the Son of Man will come."

Take a moment and think about your life and the four precepts of the Catholic faith.

1. You shall attend Mass on Sundays and on Holy Days of Obligation and rest from servile labor.

2. You shall confess your sins at least once a year.

3. You shall receive the sacrament of the Eucharist at least once during the Easter season.

4. You shall observe the days of fasting and abstinence established by the Church.

5. You shall help to provide for the needs of the Church.

EXERCISE – How are you doing with:

#1 _____

#2 _____

#3 _____

#4 _____

#5 _____

Let us pray,

Lord,

I do love You and I desire to love You all the more.

Help me to remain wide awake in my life of faith.

Help me to keep my eyes on You through all things so that I am always prepared for You when You come to me.

Jesus, I trust in You.

Amen.

Use this section below to journal any thoughts or inspirations from the meditation to help with further reflection.

Day 78

Simplicity versus Laziness

"Simplicity" is a word with an almost magical ring to it; if we could just simplify our lives, we think, it would solve many of our problems. Yet we often go about the simplification process in the wrong way.

While simplifying is largely associated with doing less, this is an impoverished definition of the idea. Monks embody simplicity, and while they do far fewer worldly things, they do far more study, worship, prayer, and so on.

In fact, there is no such thing as doing less overall; doing less of one thing always means doing more of another. If you reduce the time you spend on social/community/work engagements, you may expand the time you spend watching Netflix.

What we often really do in the name of simplification, then, is to decrease activities that require effort, while increasing those that don't. Yet this can just be a more flattering way of describing laziness — and actually, conflict with our stated aim of simplicity.

If, for example, you hope to have a memorable, enchanted holiday season, and yet jettison all the traditions and activities that would create such, then your aspirations and your actions are working at cross-purposes; your life is divided and conflicted — not simple.

Real simplicity means having a purpose and then prioritizing your life around it. That may indeed require doing less of that which detracts from your purpose, but it can also necessitate doing more of that which contributes to it. The goal is to have every element in your life work in harmony towards your aims.

By all means, ruthlessly cut out those commitments that don't contribute to your desires, but ensure that which fills the gap does. The simple life is not a matter of sheer amounts, nor of the magnitude of effort, but of wholeness and integrity.

EXERCISE – How can you simplify your life without becoming lazy?

1. _____
2. _____
3. _____
4. _____
5. _____

MEDITATION:

"Those who are able thus to enclose themselves within the little heaven of their soul where dwells the Creator of both heaven and earth, and who can accustom themselves not to look at anything nor to remain in any place which would preoccupy their exterior senses, may feel sure that they are traveling by an excellent way, and that they will certainly attain to drink of the water from the fountain, for they will journey far in a short time" (Saint Teresa of Avila)

Use this section below to journal any thoughts or inspirations from the meditation to help with further reflection.

Day 79

The Seventh Commandment – Thou shall not steal.

The Seventh Commandment forbids unjustly taking or keeping the goods of one's neighbor and wronging him in any way with respect to his goods. It commands justice and charity in the care of earthly goods and the fruits of men's labor. For the sake of the common good, it requires respect for the universal destination of goods and respect for the right to private property. Christian life strives to order this world's goods to God and to fraternal charity.

The following list contains questions to help with your discernment of the Seventh Commandment and your life. Have you:

- Stolen? (Taken something that doesn't belong to me against the reasonable will of the owner.)
- Envied others on account of their possessions?
- Neglected to live in a spirit of gospel poverty and simplicity?
- Neglected to give generously to others in need?
- Not considered that God has provided me with money so that I might use it to benefit others, as well as for my own legitimate needs?
- Allowed myself to be conformed to a consumer mentality (buy, buy, buy, throw away, waste, spend, spend, spend?)
- Neglected to practice the corporal works of mercy?
- Deliberately defaced, destroyed, or lost another's property?
- Cheated on a test, taxes, sports, games, or in business?
- Squandered money in compulsive gambling?
- Make a false claim to an insurance company?
- Paid my employees a living wage, or failed to give a full day's work for a full day's pay?

- Failed to honor my part of a contract?
- Failed to make good on a debt?
- Overcharge someone, especially to take advantage of another's hardship or ignorance?
- Misused natural resources?

Let us pray,

Eternal Savior,

I acknowledge my sin to You today and I will no longer cover up my iniquity.

The enemy wants to use my sins and shame to keep me away from You, but I will confess my transgressions to You, and I know that You will forgive the guilt of my sin.

Thank You for Your divine forgiveness that comes only from You!

Thank You for getting rid of the shame that the enemy wants me to feel trapped in.

There is none like You Lord,

Amen.

Use this section below to journal any thoughts or inspirations from the meditation to help with further reflection.

_____

_____

_____

_____

_____

_____

_____

_____

_____

_____

_____

_____

Day 80

Sleep

Why do we need sleep? People who can get by on four hours of sleep sometimes brag about their strength and endurance. But recent scientific studies show that a lack of sleep causes many significant changes in the body and increases your risk for serious health concerns such as obesity, disease, and even early death. Sleep is an important function for many reasons. When you sleep, your brain signals your body to release hormones and compounds that help:

- decrease risk for adverse health conditions
- manage your hunger levels
- maintain your immune system
- retain memory

But you can't catch up or makeup loss of sleep. In fact, consistently sleeping more than six to eight hours a night can negatively impact your health. The healthy amount of sleep for the average adult is around seven to eight hours each night. Those who generally slept for less than five to seven hours a night were 12 percent more likely to experience a premature death. People who slept more than eight or nine hours per night had an even higher risk — 30 percent.

Researchers also found that people who reduced their nightly sleep time from seven to eight hours to below seven hours were at an increased risk of death from all causes. Additionally, the researchers also saw an increased risk of death from all causes in those who slept for a long amount of time per night.

Sleep helps manage your appetite. Poor sleep habits can increase the body's energy needs. At night, movement and the need for calories are reduced. But when you are sleep-deprived, your brain will release chemicals to signal hunger. This can lead to eating more, exercising less, and gaining weight.

Sleep helps your immune system function. When you sleep, your immune system releases compounds called cytokines. Some cytokines have a protective effect on your immune system by helping it to fight inflammation, including inflammation due to infection. Without enough sleep, you may not have enough cytokines to keep you from getting sick. Other components of the immune system, like antibodies and white blood cells, can be reduced over time without enough sleep.

Sleep helps your memory. In addition to helping you focus, sleep helps protect and strengthen your memory. Research shows that sleeping after learning can help with memory retention. Sleep is also thought to reduce interference from external events.

People who are sleep-deprived:

- have a harder time receiving information due to the brain's overworked or fatigued neurons.
- may interpret events differently.
- tend to have impaired judgment.
- lose their ability to access previous information.

It's important to get seven to eight hours of sleep so that you can experience all the sleep stages. No one stage is responsible for memory and learning. Two stages (rapid eye movement and slow-wave sleep) contribute to:

- creative thinking
- procedural memory
- long-term memory
- memory processing

Sleep is a habit, just like eating healthy and exercise. While everyone misses a few hours of sleep sometimes, chronic lack of sleep is part of an unhealthy lifestyle and can increase your risk for serious health concerns.

Day 81

Positive Thinking

It was once said that we can create the world we live in. At any given time, we are surrounded by numerous good, bad and evil things in this world. It is important to be aware and cognizant of the reality of the world and what surrounds us, especially when it comes to our safety and the safety of our families. However, we do have a choice of what it is that we chose to focus on. We have the ability to fill our minds and our thoughts with all that is good in the world or all that is less than good. Some have said that what we see in life is a direct reflection of how we see ourselves. If a person is unhappy, depressed, and has a true dislike of themselves, they will usually see similar things in the world. The opposite is also true for the person who is happy, content, and full of love, they will usually see those similar things in the world.

Prayer can help us to see what is good and positive in the world. When we turn our gaze away from ourselves and those things of the world that are less than perfect, and onto God who is perfect, we can begin to see the beauty of His creation. As we ask God to help us see things in such a way that He can see things, we can usually begin to see the good in almost everything. There are very few things in life that a completely one way or another. No one person or thing is completely bad, everyone has some good in them. God created man in His image and what he created was good.

As we choose to see what is good and holy around us, we begin to fill our thoughts and our minds with things of beauty. The more we fill ourselves with such wonderful things we can't help but be affected by them and we, in turn, become even more beautiful. Our thoughts do have the ability to change our mood and our outlook on life.

Let's take a few minutes and reflect upon the world around us and to identify some of those things that are filled with God's beauty.

EXERCISE – List five things or people that are a reflection of what is good and beautiful.

1. _____
2. _____
3. _____
4. _____
5. _____

Let us pray,

Father You are so beautiful, and the source of all true beauty.

Your beauty emanates from Your holiness and so is integral to Your glorious nature and presence.

We see this in Your instructions to Israel to praise and worship "the beauty of holiness".

Lord, we are so thankful that You sent Your son Jesus to earth, to allow us to be made holy and thereby "beautified with salvation".

We see that it has been Your earnest desire throughout history to bestow Your beauty and splendor on a people set apart to Yourself.

We are humbled and amazed that You the God of Heaven should desire to share Your glory with created beings.

Thank you, Father, for giving us "beauty for ashes, the oil of joy for mourning, and the garments of praise for the spirit of heaviness".

As the "planting of the Lord" our hearts cry is that You may be glorified.

To that end, we constantly "meditate on the glorious splendor of Your majesty", that through beholding You and clothing ourselves with Christ, Your beauty may be perfected in us.

We also choose to take your beauty to others, as the "beautiful feet" who proclaim the good news of Your salvation, and in so doing, partner with You in bringing many sons to glory.

We do love You, Lord.

Amen.

Day 82

A Meal with Friends

There is something special about sitting down with friends for a special meal. It is even more special to have the meal with others invited into your own home. By inviting people into your home allows them entrance into your personal life. Our homes are our sacred, safe, and the most personal of places. When we invite others over, we are saying that we trust them enough and care for them enough to allow them to come close. Additionally, when we sit down and share a meal we are further connecting with others on an intimate level. Feeding our bodies with food and feeling our inner desire for connection at the same time.

Just like how our homes are a personal reflection of who we are spiritually, mentally, ethically, and morally, sitting down to share a meal also reflects who we are in the sense that eating together also includes visiting and sharing of ourselves in an intimate way with others. Having a person enter your home and to host them with a shared meal means that you are allowing that person the opportunity to see you in a very deep and transparent way.

After having a shared experience, like a meal with a friend in your home, it is easy to see how the relationship has grown. That special time together, eating, laughing, telling stories, and even confiding in each other can be transformational in so many ways. These encounters allow the opportunity for individuals to reveal aspects of who they are with one another and to be accepted, valued, and honored with that dignity that God desires for all people.

Our lives can become so busy with chores, distractions, and even obligations. Moving at such a fast pace often contributes to superficiality in relationships and even a degree of self-centeredness. Yet, making the effort to slow down and catering to the needs of another by hosting them for a special meal at your home can counteract that worldly business.

There are many scriptural references to the sharing of meals and of the importance. A few are as follows:

- So, whether you eat or drink, or whatever you do, do all to the glory of God. (1 Corinthians 10:31)
- Go, eat your bread with joy, and drink your wine with a merry heart, for God has already approved what you do. (Ecclesiastes 9:7)
- Give, and it will be given to you. Good measure, pressed down, shaken together, running over, will be put into your lap. For with the measure you use it will be measured back to you." (Luke 6:38)
- Is it not to share your bread with the hungry and bring the homeless poor into your house; when you see the naked, to cover him, and not to hide yourself from your own flesh? (Isaiah 58:7)

CHALLENGE – Plan to invite a person, a couple, or a few friends into your home for a special meal and time together. Who might you want to invite?

1. _____
2. _____
3. _____

Let us pray,

Loving Father,

we thank You for bringing us together for this meal:

may we continue to live in Your friendship and in harmony with one another.

Bless this food, a sign of Your loving care for us, and bless us in our daily lives.

Bless Your Church throughout the world, and all those who seek to do Your will today.

Bless those who are without food today, nourish their souls and care for them.

Bless those who will end their earthly journey today and welcome them into your heavenly kingdom.

Amen.

Day 83

Understanding Suffering

Why is there suffering? Why does God allow suffering?

There is one person who stands out above all to give an answer to these deepest of questions, namely St. Paul. In St. Paul's writings we find a greatly developed meaning of suffering. Saint Pope John Paul II explains why St. Paul writes so much on suffering: "The Apostle shares his own discovery and rejoices in it because of all those whom it can help – just as it helped him – to understand the salvific meaning of suffering" (Salvifici Doloris, 1).

Paul understands that the suffering he endures serves as a way to be like Christ, as well as it being for Christ's sake. Paul says: "Indeed I count everything as loss because of the surpassing worth of knowing Christ Jesus my Lord. For his sake I have suffered the loss of all things, and count them as refuse, in order that I may gain Christ and be found in him, not having a righteousness of my own, based on law, but that which is through faith in Christ, the righteousness from God depends on faith; that I may know him and the power of his resurrection, and may share his suffering, becoming like him in his death, that if possible I may attain the resurrection from the dead" (Philippians 3:8-11).

This passage follows a text where Paul speaks about all he had gained according to the flesh, being a Hebrew and a Pharisee. However, he now considers this gain to be loss and refuse, compared to gaining Christ through his sufferings. He gains righteousness not through his own power but through Christ's. Suffering is a participation in the mystery of Christ and is the way Paul can become like Christ. Suffering is his way of "becoming like him (Christ) in his death" so that he "may attain the resurrection from the dead" (Philippians 3:10-11). Through his suffering, Paul sees himself as participating in the Passion of Christ. Because we are being saved through the death and resurrection of Christ, we must participate in his Passion to obtain salvation. For Paul to live is gain because while he suffers in this life, he is imitating Christ and becoming more Christ-like. Further, to live is to gain because while Paul lives, he can spread the faith and be an example for the Christian community. He says, "But to remain in the flesh is more necessary on your account." (Philippians 1:24) Also, to die is to gain because if he were to die, he would share in the resurrection of Christ. So, whether he lives and suffers, leading to the resurrection for himself and others, or dies and shares in the resurrection himself alone, he will be united to Christ and be an example for all.

Another dimension of Paul's thought on the meaning of suffering is his conception of suffering as a means for sanctification, keeping pride at a minimum and trust in God at a maximum. He says: "And to keep me from being too elated by the abundance of revelations, a thorn was given me in the flesh, a messenger of Satan, to harass me, to keep me from being too elated. Three times I besought the Lord about this, that it should leave me; but he said to me, 'My grace is sufficient for you, for my power is made perfect in weakness.'…For the sake of Christ, then, I am content with weaknesses, insults, hardships, persecutions, and calamities; for when I am weak then I am strong" (2 Corinthians 12:7-10).

It is in weakness that we are more apt to trust in Christ because we realize that what we accomplish is not of our own doing, but the grace of Christ is working in us. Furthermore, it is in our weakness and suffering that we grow in humility and cannot pride ourselves in our accomplishments. We suffer "to make us rely, not on ourselves but on God who raises the dead." (2 Corinthians 1:9).

We see in these verses of 2 Corinthians 12 that this suffering is once again "for the sake of Christ." It is through grace that Paul can be content with suffering. We receive here an insight into the effectiveness of grace. Grace helps us to participate in the salvific act of suffering and to be content with it.

This is why Paul can say in his letter to the Galatians that "I have been crucified with Christ; it is no longer I who live, but Christ who lives in me…who loved me and gave himself up for me." (2:20) Christ gave himself up for us in the salvific act of his Passion and death; Paul sees himself doing the same in participating in the Passion and death of Christ. Christ lives in him when he is "crucified with Christ." John Paul II notes that "Christ also becomes in a particular way united to the man, Paul, through the cross" (SD, 20).

Paul reveals to us the paradox of the cross. To be crucified usually means death, but for Paul, it means Christ living in him. In suffering, when united to Christ, death now means life. This is why he says in 1 Corinthians: "For the word of the cross is folly to those who are perishing, but to us who are being saved it is the power of God" (1:18).

There is this intimate bond between the cross, the epitome of the sufferings of Christ, and the suffering of the people which is a participation in the self-same cross. Thus, participation in the cross through suffering is a way of obtaining grace, the power of God to participate in salvation. This is also why Paul can say elsewhere in Galatians: "Far be it from me to glory except in the cross of our Lord Jesus Christ, by which the world has been crucified to me, and I to the world…Henceforth let no man trouble me, for I bear on my body the marks of Jesus" (6:14, 17).

(From CNA - Brian Pizzalato)

100 days to Freedom

Day 84

Congratulations, you have made it to day 84 (12 weeks). This is a good time to stop, take a deep breath, and to evaluate how well, or maybe how not so well, the disciplines are going. Please take a minute, break out a pen or pencil, and complete this very important self-evaluation regarding adherence.

Spiritual	1 No Action	2 Almost none	3 Hit and miss	4 Almost perfect	5 Nailed it!
Daily Mass or Daily Mass readings and Spiritual Communion					
Daily Rosary					
Formal Examination of Conscience nightly					
Daily Spiritual reading					
Weekly adoration in front of the Blessed Sacrament					
Monthly Confession					

Physical	1 No Action	2 Almost none	3 Hit and miss	4 Almost perfect	5 Nailed it!
Walk or Run daily					
Push-ups / Sit-ups / Lunges daily or weight lifting					
Stretches daily					
7-8 hours' sleep a night					

Nutrition	1 No Action	2 Almost none	3 Hit and miss	4 Almost perfect	5 Nailed it!
2-3 meals a day - No eating between meals					
No candy / desserts					
No fast-food					
Fasting on Mon / Wed / Friday					

Self-Denial	1 No Action	2 Almost none	3 Hit and miss	4 Almost perfect	5 Nailed it!
No major purchases (Toiletries and needed items only)					
No TV or movies					
No social media					
No Alcohol					

Well, how did you do? Let me guess, maybe less than perfect? Join the club, I have yet to meet the perfect human or the one who completed the entire *100 days to Freedom* program without missing a discipline even once. That makes you normal, human, and maybe a little less than a superhero. Yet, as Christians, we are called toward a path of perfection, a life of holiness, a life in which we journey closer and closer to God.

The structure of this program will allow each of us to grow, to grow in virtue, character, self-discipline, and in relationship with God. Reflect once again on the scores you gave yourself above and then on the categories: Spiritual Life, Physical Health, Nutritional Health, and Self-Discipline. If you identify an area where there is more opportunity for growth, then try to place a greater focus on that area for the next week.

We have all been created in God's image and likeness, and we have been created as unique individuals. No two journeys are alike, just like no two scorecards are exactly alike. God is working in us in the exact way He feels that He needs to work in us to help us to travel our unique journey. Let go and allow Him to drive this journey. Our part is to be open to His promptings and respond when He calls.

Keep up the good work and as you progress day-by-day be prepared to enjoy the rewards that God has ready for you. Whenever we turn our focus away from ourselves and upon the Lord, we begin to realize what freedom truly feels and looks like.

Let us pray,

Father, look upon our weakness and reach out to help us with Your loving power.
You redeem us and make us Your children in Christ.
Look upon us, give us true freedom and bring us to the inheritance You promised.
We ask this through our Lord Jesus Christ, Your Son,
who lives and reigns with You and the Holy Spirit,
one God, forever and ever. Amen.

Day 85

A Day of Rest

At times we find ourselves completed exhausted. Maybe it is from the repetition of work, or study, or those extra things that pile up in life. It might even have to do with the worry and stress in our lives. Preferable our days of rest should be on Sundays as God has prescribed, but we might find that our Sundays might also have obligations that prevent a complete rest. Occasionally, we might need to take a day of rest where we remove ourselves from the stress and responsibilities of life, at least temporarily. Some call these days "Mental Health" days and call off work to stay home and regroup. The person isn't actually sick per se but does have a need for rest. One shouldn't feel guilty about taking a mental health day from time to time. However, if one finds a need to do this too often then there might be a need to evaluate their life to see how there can be more balance or better support.

A single day of rest can make all the difference by adding extra sleep, relaxation, time to think and pray without distraction, and to catch up on some of those things that there is never enough time to complete. It is also a time to evaluate what is actually important in life and how a re-prioritization might be needed.

Come to Me, all of you who are weary and carry heavy burdens,
and I will give you rest.
Take My yoke upon you.
Let Me teach you, because I am humble and gentle at heart,
and you will find rest for your souls.
For My yoke is easy to bear, and the burden I give you is light.
Matthew 11:28–30

We all need an extra day of rest from time to time.

EXERCISE –

How can you tell when you might need an extra day of rest?

1. _____
2. _____
3. _____
4. _____
5. _____

What would you do on your extra day of rest?

1. _____
2. _____
3. _____
4. _____
5. _____

Let us pray,

Jesus, I am weary.
I spend each day busy but feel I accomplish little.
Help me to set healthy boundaries and prioritize by Your Holy Spirit. I have my to-do list,
but what do You have for me today?
Help me not to miss Your divine appointments.
Set my focus on things above and keep my eyes on You.
Reveal to me what I should hold on to, and what I need to let go.
Empower and equip me for the work You have for me.
Give me the lasting strength of abiding in You.
Renew my mind, body, and spirit, Lord, and make me whole.
Amen.

Day 86

Catholic Joy

Many have asked about "Catholic Joy" and where it comes from and what is it all about. To truly understand the joy experienced by Catholics who have embraced their faith we must first understand a few things.

When we truly acknowledge our faults, our inequities, our shortcomings, and realize just how poor we actually are; and when we reach out for Him (Christ), the one who has been faithfully waiting for us to respond, then and only then, our world begins to change. A transformation begins. Something so very special is set into motion. He hears our thoughts, our prayers, and then He begins to shine His light onto us during our hours of desperation. He begins to fill us with wisdom and peace in places where there has only been confusion. He begins to show us the tiniest ways to begin to unravel the knots that we have wrapped around us through repeated bad choices and sinfulness. However, we have to reach out for Him, we must look in His direction for our answers. Yes, this seems so very simple, but not unlike John, we might also experience doubts at times. We might question our faith, especially when we are frightened, hurt, and worn down by trial after trial. Honestly: haven't we all questioned, either in our thoughts or at least in our actions: Are you the one? Should we be looking somewhere else? And how many of us, have and are still looking somewhere else for the answers?

How many of us are seeking peace, joy, and love in all the wrong places?

How many of us seek love, but settle for lust?

How many of us seek joy, but settle for cheap pleasure?

Seek satisfaction, but instead, merely feed our greed?

Seek wisdom, but then listen to fools?

Seek true beauty, but instead, latch onto what only makes us uglier?

Seek intimacy, but settle for less?

Yet, as we reach out for God, choose to look toward him for the answers, we are then touched by a ray of light, a grace, a sense of warmth, an idea, an understanding, a promise of hope and wonder that is Christ, the Christ that is the One! We begin to yearn and hunger for what is pure and true. We begin to make changes in our lives; we throw away the lies and deceptions as we come clean with the Sacrament of Confession. We suddenly discover within ourselves the ability to make choices that are different from what we had been accustomed to, in that lost cycle of habit. Our behaviors begin to change, we begin to meet new friends, we begin to grow closer to God, to the Church, and then, all of a sudden, we find a deeper meaning and understanding in the liturgy, the Mass. We begin to see our participation with heaven and the spiritual world. We progressively transform into the person that we were created by God to be. We experience love, joy, and peace. We see beauty where we had never noticed it before. We find ourselves drawn to Scripture, because maybe for the first time, it now becomes alive, and directly speaks to us. As we receive communion, the Eucharist that we receive burns within us as we truly realize Who we just consumed. We begin to taste in our lives the fruits of the Spirit that Saint Paul spoke of: Love, Joy, Peace, and Patience. We become kind and generous. This all begins as we have chosen to turn to God, to Christ for the answers.

Let us pray,

Heavenly Father,
Thank you that you are the source of all true joy in life.
Your word says that everything God created is good, and nothing is to be rejected if it is received with thanksgiving, because it is consecrated by the word of God and prayer.
Please help me to receive all the good gifts you give me with thanksgiving and gratitude in my heart.
You have loved me and have freed me from my sins by Jesus' blood.
To you be glory and dominion forever and ever.
Through Jesus Christ our Lord,
Amen.

Day 87

The Eighth Commandment - You shall not bear false witness against your neighbor.

The Eighth Commandment forbids misrepresenting the truth in our relations with others. This moral prescription flows from the vocation of the holy people to bear witness to their God who is the truth and wills the truth. Offenses against the truth express by word or deed a refusal to commit oneself to moral uprightness; they are fundamental infidelities to God and, in this sense, they undermine the foundations of the covenant. (CATECHISM OF THE CATHOLIC CHURCH, 2464)

St. Augustine teaches, "A lie consists in speaking a falsehood with the intention of deceiving."

Lying is the most direct offense against the truth. To lie is to speak or act against the truth in order to lead someone into error. By injuring a man's relation to truth and to his neighbor, a lie offends against the fundamental relation of a man and of his word to the Lord. (CATECHISM OF THE CATHOLIC CHURCH, 2483) St. Thomas Aquinas distinguishes among three types of lies.

- The first is the officious lie, told for convenience, in which no one is harmed. Here we might think of the excuses we invent for turning down an invitation we do not wish to accept, or (in past times, when a simpler world relied on more primitive telecommunications) a parent's instructing a child to tell a telephone solicitor, "I'm sorry, my parents aren't home."
- The second sort of lie is the jocose, told for amusement, or in which one exaggerates: "The fish was this big."
- The third sort of lie, the meretricious, is a true lie. Such a lie generally provides the teller no benefit but does harm to the person to or about whom it is told. The serpent's lie to Eve is a perfect illustration of this sort of lie. No one will be surprised to learn we judge the gravity of a lie by the

quality of the truth it distorts, the intentions of the individual who tells the lie, and the ills suffered by those against whom the lie is told.

THE REMEDY FOR LYING

Regard for truth means we must take practical steps to repair any damage we may have done by lying. If the lie was public, the reparation ought to be public. In addition, if the individual suffered harm because of a lie, she or he should be compensated for it in some way. An apology is a good place to begin the process of amendment and is the very smallest step we can take to restore the justice and charity that ought to characterize our relations with one another.

THE VALUE OF SILENCE

While we may never lie about another person, or about a particular situation or event, we may not always be obliged to share whatever truth we may know. Priests, for example, may never reveal what they have heard in the Sacrament of Reconciliation. Doctors, lawyers, and other professionals are bound, to some extent, by similar codes. The Catechism expresses what ought to be no more than common sense when it states:

> Charity and respect for the truth should dictate the response to every request for information or communication. The good and safety of others, respect for privacy, and the common good are sufficient reasons for being silent about what ought not be known or for making use of a discreet language. The duty to avoid scandal often commands strict discretion. No one is bound to reveal the truth to someone who does not have the right to know it. (CATECHISM OF THE CATHOLIC CHURCH, 2489)

Let us pray,

Lord Jesus Christ!
Thou Son of God and Son of the Virgin Mary, God and Man, Thou who in fear sweated blood for us on the Mount of Olives in order to bring peace, and to offer Thy Most Holy Death to God Thy Heavenly Father for the salvation of this dying person.
If it be, however, that by his sins he merits eternal damnation, then may it be deflected from him.
This, O Eternal Father through Our Lord Jesus Christ, Thy Dear Son, Who liveth and reigneth in union with the Holy Spirit now and forever.
Amen.

100 days to Freedom

Day 88

Where is Your Emmaus

The disciples were heading to Emmaus. Where is Emmaus, you might ask? It is a place just seven miles from Jerusalem. Why were they going to Emmaus? Because it is just seven miles from Jerusalem, and if you were walking, it is just far enough to get away from the misery and confusion of Jerusalem. The writer Frederick Buechner describes Emmaus well, *Emmaus is whatever we do, or wherever we go to make ourselves forget that the world holds nothing sacred: that even the wisest, bravest, and loveliest, decay and die; that even the noblest ideas that we have had – ideas about love and freedom and justice – have always in time been twisted out of shape by selfish men for selfish ends.*

We all have an Emmaus! For some, it is the Adoration room. For some, it is being absorbed into a good novel. For some, it is spending time with grandchildren. For others, it is outdoors. Whether hiking a trail, kayaking the river, or camping in the forest, some escape the misery and confusion often found in this world. And that is where Jesus found these two disciples, going to a place where they could sort through the pain of Christ's death, and the confusion of the rumors floating around that maybe He wasn't dead after all.

Then Jesus approached the disciples as a stranger, and his mood didn't match their own. He was informal and maybe even a little chatty, stating, "Whatch y'all talking about?" The disciples looked at Him, filled with several kinds of sadness, apparently also a little irritated at the ignorance of the stranger, and responded, "What hole did you just crawl out of? Everyone knows what has been happening in Jerusalem." Then the disciples began to tell the stranger all about Jesus, His death, and the rumors of His resurrection. But Jesus rebuked them for being so reluctant to believe, and to prove His point, He began explaining the Scripture. How he pointed toward that very moment in time, and even though they listened, they didn't hear Him. And even though He was at their side, walking with them, they didn't see Him. As the travelers approached their destination, Jesus, who always seemed to be several steps ahead of the disciples, walked on as if to continue His journey. He didn't want to impose on the hospitality of the disciples or to force Himself into their still-mourning hearts. But the disciples urged Him to stay.

Now the scene begins to change. The strange traveler, their honored guest, had been given a spot at the head of the table. As they prepared to eat, He followed a formula that He had used before and that we have been using in the Church ever since. He took the bread, broke it, blessed it, and gave it to the disciples. That was what they needed, and with that, their eyes were opened. And when the disciples finally realized and recognized Jesus, He disappeared! Surely the disciples would have wanted Him to stay with them: they wanted to understand the mystery of His resurrection. They still had more questions, and they wanted Him in their midst because there was something so wonderful and indescribable about Him, something that filled the empty places within their hearts. So, what can we glean from this message? Jesus is always present in our lives, but we often fail to see him.

It is often looking back on the past events of our day, or a week, even our year that we can begin to see that He has touched us. He will reveal Himself in different ways to different people. But He does reveal himself. We do not have the power or the ability to force this revelation, but we can search for ways to feel His presence and to celebrate Him.

EXERCISE – Reflecting back on your week, year, and even decade, how has Jesus revealed Himself to you?

1. _____
2. _____
3. _____
4. _____
5. _____

Let us pray,

O my God, I firmly believe that Thou art one God, in three Divine Persons, the Father, the Son and the Holy Ghost; I believe that Thy Divine Son became man and died for our sins and that He will come to judge the living and the dead. I believe these and all the truths which the holy Catholic Church teaches, because Thou hast revealed them, Who canst neither deceive nor be deceived. Amen.

100 days to Freedom

Day 89

Who Is My Neighbor?

In the time of Jesus, the rabbis determined that there were 613 separate laws in the five books of Moses, and they believed that if they could fulfill them all, God would grant them eternal life. Quite a daunting task, because just to know and understand those laws, one would need a lifetime of study. And, if this were true for the highly educated rabbis, what about the common folk who couldn't even read and write? And so, the Hebrew teachers set out to identify which laws were the greatest, which laws summed up the entire Mosaic code so that if one were to fulfill those particular laws, one would fulfill them all. It was a question that was posed to Jesus probably on several occasions, because He was seen as a great rabbi, and when He was challenged by a scholar of the law, we learn that the law of God can be summed up in two commands:

- You shall love the Lord God with all your heart, with all your being, with all your strength, and with all your mind.
- And to love your neighbor as yourself.

Love of God and love of neighbor contain all the laws of the prophets, and if we do this, we will have life. Why? Because if we love God perfectly, with our whole being, we will fulfill our whole duty toward others by recognizing in everyone we meet a person equal in dignity to ourselves, created in God's image, redeemed by the blood of His only son. We would never want to harm such persons, and we would always seek to help them in their need. But the scholar is not satisfied with this answer and wants to engage Jesus in a rabbinical debate, he interrogates Him further, questioning "And who is my neighbor? Who am I obligated to Love?" The question is the same question that we should be asking of ourselves, who is my neighbor? Who must I show love, care, compassion, and forgiveness? Who must I show unconditional friendship? As an unsigned Check is of no value to us, Charity (Good Thoughts) without action towards our neighbor is also of no value. Good thoughts without action will not accumulate treasures in heaven.

Let us look at some of our neighbors and our obligations toward them.

1. First, let's look at the obligation of parents and godparents to raise their children is the sound doctrines of the Catholic faith.

2. Let us also consider the situation of the homeless. There are many in our communities who are found sleeping in parks, behind stores, and along the river. Where are the Catholics who are reaching out to them? How many of us have personally helped them to wash themselves, do their laundry, give them extra clothing, or even a little food to sustain them for even a few days? Or do we rationalize an excuse?

3. What about those who are hungry? Are we reaching out to support the large families by proving them with a little extra food? Are we reaching out to those who are out of work, those who just don't have the means to meet their basic needs? What about the seniors around us?

4. What about the persecuted? Do we speak up when we see someone bullied? Do we speak up when we hear of prejudice? Do we speak up when we see minors showing disrespect towards elders? Do we speak up when we hear others gossip and destroy reputations?

5. What about the prisoners, are they not also our neighbors? Yes, even if we do not want to hear about it, the prisoners are also our neighbors. Believe it or not, that includes murderers, rapists, and the child molesters. To exclude these as our neighbors, it is to be dishonest to ourselves by rejecting the message of our Lord Jesus Christ. If we neglect the salvation of these souls by refusing to share the gospel of Christ with them, who then will bring them the good news of the kingdom of God?

6. What about the prostitutes on the streets, some of them being so young that it is shameful to just think about it? Who is reaching out to these young girls? Are we ready to help those girls who have run away from home for whatever reason? How many of them were raped before they turned to prostitution? How many of them are selling their bodies because their pimps are providing them with food, shelter, and false love?

7. How about the single parents and widows who must bear the burden alone of raising their children? Are we there for them as Good Samaritans? Are we offering our services as babysitters so they can get an hour off here and there? Are we offering our assistance with cooking or housecleaning?

8. And finally, what about all these young girls who are considering an abortion? Are we there for them? Are we there to help them through their pregnancy? Are we ready to commit ourselves to help them raise their children? Are we willing to walk that extra mile to save an unborn child and the soul of its mother?

100 days to Freedom

Day 90

Mastering Moderation

We are now heading into the homestretch of the *100 days to Freedom* program. There have been many disciplines that you have adhered to, and for some the structure of the program has made life simple. The completed disciplines we structured to be temporary, although many of them you might want to keep in your everyday lives. If you have not relaxed the disciplines on Sundays it is now time to do so. This slight relaxation of the disciplines is structured to help you ease back into "Normal" life while still experiencing moderation and control over your vices. Do not be surprised if you are tempted toward excess or gluttony since we have a tendency to do so, remember our concupiscence? If you overdo it, learn from that experience. If it was overeating, over-drinking, overspending, whatever. Sticking to a program is easy for many people, it is learning to live in moderation that many people struggle with. Remember, you are not doing this alone, God is present. If you begin to feel tempted beyond what you feel capable of handling, or you see yourself failing, increase your prayers. Do not forget all that you have learned over the past three months. You have learned to rely on God and you also learned that God uses everything, even our failures to help us grow in virtue.

Take a few minutes to plan how you will relax the disciplines on Sunday. Having a plan is the first step in remaining in control. List five ways you are going to enjoy Sunday while relaxing your disciplines.

1. _____
2. _____
3. _____
4. _____
5. _____

100 days to Freedom

As you have traveled the journey of freedom and have experienced the numerous disciplines of the program, there has more than likely been a few of the disciplines that you have identified that have been transformational for you. Some of these disciplines are things that you will want to continue after the program has completed. Take a minute and list a few disciplines that you feel will be something that you see benefit in making a part of your ongoing life.

1. _____
2. _____
3. _____
4. _____
5. _____

Let us pray,

Dear God,

Please help me to have more self-control.

Train me, Lord, like an athlete to be strong and determined.

Feed me with your truth in Scripture to make me healthy.

May I exercise muscles of forgiveness, patience, and peacemaking.

Lord, increase my stamina to give out to those in need.

And may I be freed from past hurts and confusions so that I can run free.

Come fill my life with your resurrection hope!

Amen.

Use this section below to journal any thoughts or inspirations from the meditation to help with further reflection.

_____
_____
_____
_____
_____
_____
_____

Day 91

Stewardship

Let's ask ourselves "What kind of giver am I?" Recalling a true story, there was a man who was clearly homeless and sitting on the side of the road. A parishioner walked by the homeless man and felt compelled to do something for him. He asked the homeless man, "Can I buy you a hamburger?" The homeless man reached over and grabbed a paper bag, it contained numerous hamburgers that other people had given to him. Not knowing what to say, the parishioner stated, "Is there anything I can do for you?" The homeless man responded, "I just wish someone really cared." He didn't want a handout, he wanted someone to talk to, someone to care about him. The parishioner sat down with the man, and they visited for over an hour on the sidewalk. They talked about life, happiness, sadness, faith, hopes and dreams, family, and love. They established a relationship, a friendship.

Probably the greatest gift that is often withheld is the gift of our time and attention. There are so many starving people, not starving for food or nourishment, but starving for attention, many among our own families and friends. We must ask ourselves, what kind of a giver am I? Do I only give from my surplus, or do I give my all? Let's think about the people in our own lives. What do I give to them? Is it from my surplus, or do I truly give my all to them? Do I hold back, if so, why? Is it out of fear, is it out of being selfish, why?

Let's look at our ability to give through the concept of the three T's (Time, Talent, and Treasure) How much of my time do I give? How much of my talent do I share? What treasure do I possess that I am willing to give back to God? For each of us, the determination of how and what to give will be as unique as we are.

So, what really is stewardship? Stewardship is a way of living. It is a lifestyle, a life of total accountability and responsibility. It is the acknowledging of God as the creator and the owner of all.

Christian Stewards see themselves as the caretaker of all of God's gifts. Gratitude for these many gifts is expressed in our prayer, worship, offerings, and action. Stewardship is a way of thanking God for all our blessings by returning to God a portion of the many gifts (our time, talent, and treasure) that we have been given. Stewardship is about the holistic approach and discernment of the three T's God has blessed us with. Stewardship contains action, love, trust, and faith.

REFLECTION - A missionary priest in Africa heard a knock on the door of his hut one afternoon. Opening the door, the priest found a native boy holding a large fish in his hands. The boy said "Father, you taught us what tithing is. So, I have brought you my tithe." As the Priest gratefully took the fish, he asked the boy. "If this is your tithe, where are the other nine fish?" At this, the boy with a beaming smile said, "Oh, they're still back in the river. I'm going back to catch them now." Clearly, the boy understood that all he had, all that had been and would be given to him, really came from and belonged to God.

EXERCISE – Please list how you are sharing your three T's (Time. Talent, and Treasure).

Time: _____
_____

Talent: _____
_____

Treasure: _____
_____

Day 92

Temptation

Temptations come to all of us in our lives – in various disguise of course. They are part and parcel of each of our lives. So, what is a temptation? A temptation is a trick, a deception, a lie. It conceals the truth and presents falsehood to us as the truth. A temptation may even offer us something good but entices us to use it in a false and selfish way. These temptations come from the devil, who is called the "father of lies."

In the story of Adam and Eve we hear about the perfect world God created for humans, and how through a temptation Adam established a pattern that led to sin and death. The Eden story was a drama woven of pretense and cover-up. Adam and Eve were the first to bite on a big lie: a lie that included the denial that we as creatures of God are dependent on God. The serpent, that cunning beast, that lord of lies, taunted their obedience and reliance on God. Ah, the attraction of having no limits. To be God. To be self-sufficient, self-made. The pretense was attractive, desirable. The trick looked so wise. The devil, being the master of deceit, knows human psychology only too well. His first task was to get the attention of Eve. Thus, his question, "Did God really tell you not to eat from any of the trees in the garden?" Eve right away saw the half-truth in the question so she corrected him saying that they could eat of the fruit of all the trees except that of "The Tree of the Knowledge of Good and Bad." And God's command was clear, "You shall not eat it or even touch it, lest you die." We see here how Eve, by arguing with the devil, got hooked. Then the devil took immediate advantage of his gain. He told Eve that they would not die; instead, he stated, "Your eyes will be opened, and you will be like gods who know what is good and what is bad." Her curiosity was aroused. Eve saw that the fruit was good for food, pleasing to the eye, and desirable for gaining wisdom. Eve then took fruit and ate it. She gave one to her husband Adam who likewise ate it. Then suddenly both of them realized that they were naked. Ashamed of their nakedness in front of each other, they covered parts of themselves, and now being afraid of God, they went into hiding. They had fallen and sin had entered the world!

Sin brings about a dislocation in relationships. Instead of openness – hiding or covering–up became a way of relating to God and to each other. This is not unique to Adam and Eve but is true to us as well. And sadly, we justify our weaknesses and sins with all kinds of rationalizations. And if we are honest, this story represents our life as well. But there is hope, let us now turn our attention to Jesus and the story of his temptations. After his baptism by John the Baptist at Jordan River, Jesus was led by the Spirit into the desert where he prayed and fasted for forty days and nights, and afterward, he too was tested. The testing was done not by God directly but by the Evil One, the Tempter. The three temptations of Jesus are the same three essential weapons that the devil has in his arsenal to destroy us too, humanity. The first temptation is of appetite, that being (pleasure/gluttony and materialism) – to change stones into bread. The second temptation is that of ambition (power/fame / and boasting) - to jump from the pinnacle of the Temple. The third temptation is that of arrogance (pride/vanity and idolatry) - To worship the devil who can give power and wealth. These three temptations are also our temptations, and to them, somehow, all temptations are connected. The devil invites us to turn towards self. And in contrast, Jesus invites us to turn towards God. In fact, these three tests are really symbols of the real tests that not only do we find in the life of Jesus but in our lives as well. They draw attention to our appetite, ambition, & arrogance. They speak of our desire for pleasure, power, & pride.

We must never forget that all temptations come to us under the guise of some kind of goodness. I seriously doubt that anyone here would willingly choose to do something purely evil, but we are tempted when there is a positive benefit that may come from a less than honorable action.

So, what is it that Christ is trying to teach us? We must realize that we are all on a human journey that includes fall and redemption. Like Adam and Eve, and Jesus, we all face temptations. Original sin reminds us that we humans tend to give in to temptation. It is a family trait. The mother and father of humanity did it, and we also do it. So, when we are tempted, we should not trust in our own abilities or strength, because we are sinful from our origins. How many of us had fought against temptation and lost! All of us! Instead, when confronted with a temptation we should trust in Jesus and his strength because God is gracious and has been from the beginning. Where humanity fails, Jesus prevails. So, the point is that we should follow his lead when we face temptations. We should look at how Jesus faced temptations. We should learn from his example. Then when we face the same temptations, those temptations of appetite, ambition, & arrogance, of pleasure, power and pride, which we all do, we can then resist them, and be victorious over them.

Day 93

The Ninth Commandment - Thou shall not covet thy neighbor's wife
(From the Catechism of the Catholic Church)

Everyone who looks at a woman lustfully has already committed adultery with her in his heart. St. John distinguishes three kinds of covetousness or concupiscence: lust of the flesh, lust of the eyes, and pride of life. In the Catholic catechetical tradition, the Ninth Commandment forbids carnal concupiscence; the tenth forbids coveting another's goods. Etymologically, "concupiscence" can refer to any intense form of human desire. Christian theology has given it a particular meaning: the movement of the sensitive appetite contrary to the operation of the human reason. The apostle St. Paul identifies it with the rebellion of the "flesh" against the "spirit." Concupiscence stems from the disobedience of the first sin. It unsettles man's moral faculties and, without being in itself an offense, inclines man to commit sins.

Because man is a composite being, spirit and body, there already exists a certain tension in him; a certain struggle of tendencies between "spirit" and "flesh" develops. But in fact, this struggle belongs to the heritage of sin. It is a consequence of sin and at the same time a confirmation of it. It is part of the daily experience of the spiritual battle.

PURIFICATION OF THE HEART-The heart is the seat of moral personality: "Out of the heart come evil thoughts, murder, adultery, fornication. . ." The struggle against carnal covetousness entails purifying the heart and practicing temperance: "Remain simple and innocent, and you will be like little children who do not know the evil that destroys man's life." The sixth beatitude proclaims, "Blessed are the pure in heart, for they shall see God." "Pure in heart" refers to those who have attuned their intellects and wills to the demands of God's holiness, chiefly in three areas: charity; chastity or sexual rectitude; love of truth and orthodoxy of faith. There is a connection between purity of heart, of body, and of faith. The faithful must believe the articles of the Creed "so that by believing they may obey God, by obeying may live well, by living well may purify their hearts, and with pure hearts may understand what they believe." The "pure in heart" are promised that they will see

God face to face and be like him. Purity of heart is the precondition of the vision of God. Even now it enables us to see according to God, to accept others as "neighbors"; it lets us perceive the human body - ours and our neighbor's - as a temple of the Holy Spirit, a manifestation of divine beauty.

THE BATTLE FOR PURITY - Baptism confers on its recipient the grace of purification from all sins. But the baptized must continue to struggle against concupiscence of the flesh and disordered desires. With God's grace, he will prevail:

- by the virtue and gift of chastity, for chastity lets us love with upright and undivided heart;
- by the purity of intention which consists in seeking the true end of man: with the simplicity of vision, the baptized person seeks to find and to fulfill God's will in everything;
- by the purity of vision, external and internal; by the discipline of feelings and imagination; by refusing all complicity in impure thoughts that incline us to turn aside from the path of God's Commandments: "Appearance arouses yearning in fools";
- by prayer.

Purity requires modesty, an integral part of temperance. Modesty protects the intimate center of the person. It means refusing to unveil what should remain hidden. It is ordered to chastity to whose sensitivity it bears witness. It guides how one looks at others and behaves toward them in conformity with the dignity of persons and their solidarity. Modesty protects the mystery of persons and their love. It encourages patience and moderation in loving relationships; it requires that the conditions for the definitive giving and commitment of man and woman to one another be fulfilled. Modesty is decency. It inspires one's choice of clothing. It keeps silence or reserve where there is an evident risk of unhealthy curiosity. It is discreet.

There is a modesty of the feelings as well as of the body. It protests, for example, against the voyeuristic explorations of the human body in certain advertisements, or against the solicitations of certain media that go too far in the exhibition of intimate things. Modesty inspires a way of life which makes it possible to resist the allurements of fashion and the pressures of prevailing ideologies.

The forms taken by modesty vary from one culture to another. Everywhere, however, modesty exists as an intuition of the spiritual dignity proper to man. It is born with the awakening consciousness of being a subject. Teaching modesty to children and adolescents means awakening in them respect for the human person.

Day 94

Finding Peace Through Obedience

We live in a world in which we are bombarded with influences. Influences that come to us through a variety of mediums: TV, radio, internet, what we chose to read, our friends, work, school, teachers, and parents, just to name a few. And the more we are presented with these influences, life events, and worldly situations, our brains begin to normalize whatever it is exposed to. The more we are repeatedly exposed to something, we begin to accept it as "Normal." This could be good or bad, depending on the situation and influence. A question to you is: What are the main influences in your life, and what have you come to accept as "Normal?"

We would all probably agree, that it only makes sense, that when Jesus did something, it had a purpose. Prior to leaving this world for the next, Jesus handed over the keys to the Church, His Church, to Peter, and asked Peter to guide His Church. And then like tongues of fire, God sent the Holy Spirit, the Advocate, down upon the Apostles, down upon the Magisterium, and especially down upon His Pope, to be the voice of God here on earth. Remember what Jesus proclaimed: "The Holy Spirit will teach you everything." And what is the purpose of the Holy Spirit? To build up the One, Holy, Catholic, and Apostolic Church. Visible in nature with its seat in Rome, its invisible reflection in the holy city with its seat in Jerusalem where the One, Holy, Catholic and Apostolic Church had its beginning. The unity of the two forms the mystical body of Christ, the Church, also known as the bride of Christ.

The second goal of the Holy Spirit is to sanctify us in Christ so we may be purified and transformed in the likeness of Jesus. When we turn to Rome, the teachings of the Church, and live in obedience to them, we are able to walk with the Spirit of Christ. We are able to be led not by ourselves and our own desires but are truly led by the Spirit.

A few questions to consider:

- Where do we as Catholics turn to for advice and direction?
- What or who do we allow to be influential factors in our lives?
- What behavior have we accepted as normal in our society?

Regrettably, for many, it isn't Rome, nor the Pope that they turn to for direction. In fact, they live lives in direct contrast to what the Church teaches and asks from us, yet they still call themselves Catholic. And in regard to being obedient, most are more concerned with being independent than submissive and obedient, even if it is the Holy Church, the Bride of Christ, that we are speaking of.

Why Obedience, and what does it actually do for us? Obedience brings us peace and freedom. As Jesus stated, "Peace I leave you; My peace I give to you. Not as the world gives do I give to you." To understand what peace really means, we should take a closer look at the word "Peace." Actually, the term Jesus used was not peace, but Shalom. This Hebrew word is generally translated into English as "Peace", but this is a simplistic rendering of a very rich expression. Shalom really describes completeness, wholeness, fulfillment – everything in life being as it should be. We tend to equate peace with the absence of war or conflict, but it is much more than that. Peace in our lives, in our souls, goes far deeper. It is a sincere peace that assures us that we are truly loved by God. It is not the world's peace; Jesus says it is His peace. The peace we search for is the peace that only comes from Christ. It is a peace the world cannot give us, and that we will never find if we look for it anywhere other than God. This is the peace that comes from His presence in our lives, it flows from Him. It is Jesus Himself, living and acting in us, and through us. Sometimes, it is us bringing Christ's peace, being Christ's peace, to others. The more we work, not for ourselves, but for the glory of God, the more we find peace. The more we keep Christ's word because we love Him, the more His peace will live in us, and the less our hearts will be troubled or afraid. We can see this in the lives of so many Christians who go through trials and even tragedies. Yes, they suffer, and they grieve, but they do so with a level of peace that comes to them through their faith in and love of Christ. To be obedient to the Church and her teachings is to free oneself from the burdens, temptations, and evils of the world. It is Christ himself, working through the Holy Spirit that decides what is "Normal" not the other influences in our lives.

To be Catholic means to be complete, whole, fulfilled – and having everything in life being as it should be. Jesus has shown us the way and has even left us with His Church, under the direction and guidance of a Pope, to guide, support, and love us.

The final question is: Are we embracing this gift, or throwing it away?

Day 95

Dying to Self

How loud our world has become, in the car, at home, at your desk at the office, even sitting in the church. Just about wherever we are at any given time we're confronted by sound. And it's not just sound that confronts us either, it's everything that takes hold of our thoughts and senses. Anything that demands the attention of our eyes, our appetites, our desires. Billboards on the interstate, pop-ups on our computers, and maybe most destructive of all, the thoughts that push us into the confusing mazes of our minds. Hopes, dreams, anxieties all mixed up in a never-ending deluge of thoughts. Our time is marked with the inability to break free of the noise and arrive at any kind of silence. In the end, this particular modern reality proves to be one of the greatest obstacles in our relationship with God.

Meister Eckhart, the great German Dominican from the 1300s said, "Nothing resembles the language of God so much as does silence." If this is correct then we are living in a time where the language of God is almost inaudible.

This calls to mind a story. It's the story from Fr. Henry Nouwen. Fr. Nouwen was definitely an intellectual. He had three doctorates from major universities, Harvard, Yale, and Notre Dame. He was a sought-after Spiritual Director and Retreat Master. He could've held any post he wanted in really any university in the world. Instead, he chose to go to work as the Spiritual Director at L'arche, a home for mentally handicapped people in Toronto. He recalls one evening at dinner with his new housemates, at L'arche they all ate dinner together, staff with residents. One evening at table Fr. Nouwen tried to pass the meatloaf to the person next to him to which a very confident young man from across the table interjected, "No, no, no, Father, don't pass him the meatloaf, he doesn't eat meat, he's a Presbyterian." It was at this point that Fr. Henry realized he had truly arrived at a place where his Ph.D.'s didn't matter. The fact that people from all over the world called him to lead retreats didn't matter, the fact that he could speak multiple languages didn't matter to any of his new housemates. He had finally arrived at a place where there was no need to assert his own agenda, to talk about his own accomplishments, to market his résumé. It wouldn't matter to them anyway. He explains that this was when he finally became free. Fr. Nouwen had experienced the need to die to self. Remember what Jesus said, "Whoever wishes to save his life will lose it and whoever is willing to lose his life will save it."

Dying to self is what we experienced in Father Nouwen's story. If anyone wishes to be first, he shall be the last and the servant of all. The fact remains that we have this innate, almost unquenchable need to assert ourselves, to interject our thoughts, feelings, and opinions onto the world so that we have some proof that we are in the game, that we are important, that we are essential to whatever is going on around us at a given time. We are afraid that somehow if we're quiet, if we die to self, if we humble ourselves to be last rather than first, we might not be happy. We're secretly afraid that we might not get what we so desperately want in life. And so, we are driven to make something of our lives. We grasp for any sort of way to leave our mark on the world so that we will be known and valued. Yet, we are missing Christ's teaching and his way of life by doing so, especially when it comes to faith. Faith is the antidote to the dysfunction of needing to assert oneself upon the world, upon our community, and upon our closest family and friends. Faith invites us to believe that our real significance is not to have our name put up on billboards, but rather to have our name written in heaven for eternity. And that's the beginning of sainthood.

There are two particular saints for whom this kind of faith was totally evident. St. Joseph and St. John the Baptist, both undeniably vital in salvation history. St. Joseph had he not said "yes", had he not taken in the Virgin Mary, had he not died to self, you and I would not be a Christian today. He said yes, he protected Mary and Jesus, he provided for them, it is because of him that Jesus was able to do his work. And yet, after the flight into Egypt, and the brief mention of Joseph when Jesus was teaching in the temple, we hear nothing more of him. He completely melts into the background. And John the Baptist, his whole purpose was to announce the arrival of Jesus onto the scene. He prepares the way then points him out. After the baptism of our Lord, John exits stage left. He even says so, "I must decrease and He must increase." There's no doubt about it, John the Baptist was not some weakling without a healthy ego. It was in his strength that he was able to be last and a servant to all.

Fr. Thomas Merton who says life is a battle between our real and false selves. Our false selves are the identities we cultivate in order to function in society with pride and self-possession; and our real selves are a deep religious mystery, known entirely only to God. The world cultivates the false self and ignores the real one and therein lies the great irony of our human condition: the more we try to make of ourselves the less we actually exist. Whoever wishes to save his life will lose it and whoever is willing to lose his life will save it. And If anyone wishes to be first, he shall be the last of all and servant of all.

Day 96

Mary and Elizabeth Show Us the Way

There are two very different, but profound messages given to us in the gospel and through the examples of two remarkable women; Mary and Elizabeth. Let's begin with Mary – As we all know, she was carrying Jesus within her womb and what does she do? Does she withdrawal from the community and hideaway with this treasure? No, she ventures out into the world with a plan to give service to Elizabeth. Carrying the person of Christ, His love, His grace, and His power, she sets off out into the world, allowing Christ to be present to others. Are we are applying Mary's example to our lives as well? Each week, and for some of us each day, we receive Christ through the Holy Eucharist; Body, Blood, Soul, and Divinity. He becomes as real within us as He was within Mary, and what do we do after Mass? Do we go home and hid him from the world? Or, do we, like Mary, go to great effort to share him, and show him to others?

Once asked by a group of Protestants what the main difference was between the Catholic and protestant faiths what immediately came to mind was the Sacraments, Mary, the Mass. There are share similarities, yet there were some significant differences. One of those unique and significant differences is our belief in relationships. As Catholics, our primary focus on spirituality is not just a "Me and God" relationship where it is entirely about a personal relationship with God. But rather, a common relationship, shared by a larger group of people, called to serve each other, to love each other, to care for and live for each other. You can see how there is a significant difference; one understanding is quite self-centered in the "God and me" relationship. And the other is just the opposite, it is self-less and truly sacrificial.

The other example from the gospel is that from Elizabeth, who immediately identifies and is aware of the presence of God in her midst. How many of us are able to recognize when God's spirit is upon us? How many of us can see and are aware when God places someone filled with grace into our midst? What power or ability did Elizabeth possess to so clearly see Christ, even Christ hidden within the womb? She had the same ability that we have; it is the Holy Spirit, but she was not hindered by distractions, nor obstacles that can distort so very well. One might even say that she had prepared herself well through living a good life, a holy life, a life that enabled her to truly see the world and its effects so clearly. This preparation was not unique to Elizabeth, it is the same preparation that we are all called to partake in. It has a lot to do with patience, faith, and participating with God when he acts in our lives. Elizabeth shows us that even after being barren for so many years, desiring a child, she doesn't give up hope, she perseveres, living an honorable life, caring for her husband and those around her. And when God chose to finally act, giving her a child, even in her old age, she accepts, trusts the Lord, and nourishes the gift placed into her womb. Did she boast of the miracle? No, rather instead, she remains humble and thankful; in fact, what is her initial response when Mary arrives, Elizabeth doesn't focus on herself, but rather states, "How does this happen to me that the mother of my Lord should come to me?" She possessed true humility.

When we place our focus and attention on others, and not on ourselves, our ability to see God's presence in and amongst our lives becomes so clear. When we live simple and pure lives, allowing time for contemplation, for prayer, and for serving others, this allows Gods' spirit to manifest itself completely and radiates free from selfish personal desires and self- absorbency. It is difficult to see Christ in others when we are constantly only looking at ourselves. Mary and Elizabeth have shown us through their life example, a way of embracing our Lord, a method for seeing him in and amongst our lives. It is through accepting Christ, sharing him unselfishly with others, living simple and humble lives, lives of charity and service that enables His spirit to shine. It is by following the examples of these two holy women that Christ is made visible and present in the world.

Let us pray,

Hail Mary, full of grace,
the Lord is with thee.
Blessed are thou among women,
and blessed is the fruit of thy womb, Jesus.
Holy Mary, Mother of God,
pray for us sinners, now,
and at the hour of our death.
Amen.

Day 97

Docility

In the Old Testament, we hear God speaking to Ahaz. God says, "Ask for a sign, make it as high as the sky, or as deep as the netherworld. Anything you want. Make it as outrageous as you can imagine." Ahaz, who was one of the worst kings they had ever had in Israel, suddenly becomes Mr. Pious (can you blame him, speaking to God), but says, "Oh No! I am not going to tempt God," as if he hadn't been all those years that he had been a king. Yet, God does give him, and us, a sign, so ridiculous, so impossible, and so unimaginable that it cannot be mistaken. Imagine that you were a young girl, 13, 14, or 15 years old at the most, and confronted by an angel who says, "God has chosen you to be the mother of his only begotten Son." What would you say to such a startling announcement? How would you react? The gospel shows us that Mary was greatly troubled at what was said and that she pondered the words. How many of us have been confronted with unexpected events and circumstances that seem to be beyond our understanding and our comprehension? Situations that will undoubtedly bring us grief, dishonor, pain, and humiliation? How are we expected to react to such an event? How does a faithful Catholic respond? Great question! Let's turn back to Mary for some guidance. Well, she didn't lash out in anger! She didn't strike back in retaliation; she didn't run away, she didn't pretend it didn't happen. But she was confused and frightened. At this point in her life, Mary was betrothed to Joseph but not married. In the Jewish tradition, there were three steps to a Jewish marriage: The first was "The Engagement" – This was often arranged by the parents through a matchmaker when the boy and girl were children. The second was "The Betrothal" – which was a formal ratification of the marriage-to-be, usually done a year before the couple was to be married. And the third was "The Wedding" itself – which lasted a whole week and concluded with the consummation. Mary and Joseph were betrothed, but not married yet. They had not had sexual relations and Mary was a Virgin. However, in spite of this, the Angel Gabriel said that she was to become pregnant and give birth to a son and name him Jesus. Mary was confused, and rightly so. How can this be? She had not been with a man. It doesn't make any sense. How many situations and events come into our own lives that just don't seem to make any sense as well?

- The death of an innocent child.
- The storm or fire that takes everything.
- A divorce.
- The loss of a job.
- The loss of a spouse.
- Those health issues that just won't go away!

The angel turns to Mary and says, "Do not be afraid Mary," and then declares that the Holy Spirit will come upon her and the power of the Most High will overshadow her. And what is her response? "May it be done to me according to Your will." What Faith! What Trust! What Docility! Could it be that God also gives us signs, signs that allow us to grow in faith, in trust, and in docility? Signs that at the time seem so ridiculous, so impossible, so unimaginable, so enormous that we don't know what or how to react to them? Yet, is there a purpose in those signs? Are they allowed to occur in order for us to have an opportunity to react as Mary did? Mary's "Yes" wasn't without pain. She was dishonored and ridiculed by the people of her own town. She gave birth in a dirty stable surrounded by smelly animals. She and Joseph had to flee the country in fear of their lives. She watched her only son, mocked, tortured, and murdered. Do you think she completely understood what was happening and why? I don't think so, and can you imagine the pain she must have experienced. Yet, did she even complain once! So, do we always have to know why something is occurring in order to respond in faith?

Mary's response was born out of humility and in trust in the providence of God. The good news is that such a response is also possible for all those who turn to God in faith and trust. So, the next time a situation presents itself to you, something that seems just too great to understand, too enormous to tackle, too painful to deal with, don't run away, don't ignore it, and don't try to completely understand it before you act. Act in faith, and trust, and say "May it also be done to me!" Let the Holy Spirit come upon you, and the power of the Most High overshadow you, And then, keep your eyes and your heart open to see where God is leading you, just as Mary was lead, on a journey of holiness, and a journey toward a relationship with her son, Jesus Christ, the Savior of the world.

Day 98

Congratulations, you have made it to day 98 (14 weeks). This is a good time to stop, take a deep breath, and to evaluate how well, or maybe how not so well, the disciplines are going. Please take a minute, break out a pen or pencil, and complete this very important self-evaluation regarding adherence.

Spiritual	1 No Action	2 Almost none	3 Hit and miss	4 Almost perfect	5 Nailed it!
Daily Mass or Daily Mass readings and Spiritual Communion					
Daily Rosary					
Formal Examination of Conscience nightly					
Daily Spiritual reading					
Weekly adoration in front of the Blessed Sacrament					
Monthly Confession					

Physical	1 No Action	2 Almost none	3 Hit and miss	4 Almost perfect	5 Nailed it!
Walk or Run daily					
Push-ups / Sit-ups / Lunges daily or weight lifting					
Stretches daily					
7-8 hours' sleep a night					

Nutrition	1 No Action	2 Almost none	3 Hit and miss	4 Almost perfect	5 Nailed it!
2-3 meals a day - No eating between meals					
No candy / desserts					
No fast-food					
Fasting on Mon / Wed / Friday					

Self-Denial	1 No Action	2 Almost none	3 Hit and miss	4 Almost perfect	5 Nailed it!
No major purchases (Toiletries and needed items only)					
No TV or movies					
No social media					
No alcohol					

Well, how did you do? Let me guess, maybe less than perfect? Join the club, I have yet to meet the perfect human or the one who completed the entire *100 days to Freedom* program without missing a discipline even once. That makes you normal, human, and maybe a little less than a superhero. Yet, as Christians, we are called toward a path of perfection, a life of holiness, a life in which we journey closer and closer to God.

The structure of this program will allow each of us to grow, to grow in virtue, character, self-discipline, and in relationship with God. Reflect once again on the scores you gave yourself above and then on the categories: Spiritual Life, Physical Health, Nutritional Health, and Self-Discipline. If you identify an area where there is more opportunity for growth, then try to place a greater focus on that area for the next week.

We have all been created in God's image and likeness, and we have been created as unique individuals. No two journeys are alike, just like no two scorecards are exactly alike. God is working in us in the exact way He feels that He needs to work in us to help us to travel our unique journey. Let go and allow Him to drive this journey. Our part is to be open to His promptings and respond when He calls.

Keep up the good work and as you progress day-by-day be prepared to enjoy the rewards that God has ready for you. Whenever we turn our focus away from ourselves and upon the Lord, we begin to realize what freedom truly feels and looks like.

Let us pray,

Father, look upon our weakness and reach out to help us with Your loving power.
You redeem us and make us Your children in Christ.
Look upon us, give us true freedom and bring us to the inheritance You promised.
We ask this through our Lord Jesus Christ, Your Son,
who lives and reigns with You and the Holy Spirit,
one God, forever and ever. Amen.

Day 99

The Tenth Commandment – Thou Shall Not Covet Thy Neighbor's Goods
(From the Catechism of the Catholic Church)

You shall not covet . . . anything that is your neighbor's. . . . You shall not desire your neighbor's house, his field, or his manservant, or his maidservant, or his ox, or his ass, or anything that is your neighbor's. (Ex 20:17; Deut 5:21)

For where your treasure is, there will your heart be also.

The Tenth Commandment unfolds and completes the ninth, which is concerned with concupiscence of the flesh. It forbids coveting the goods of another, as the root of theft, robbery, and fraud, which the Seventh Commandment forbids. "Lust of the eyes" leads to the violence and injustice forbidden by the Fifth Commandment. Avarice, like fornication, originates in the idolatry prohibited by the first three prescriptions of the Law. The Tenth Commandment concerns the intentions of the heart; with the ninth, it summarizes all the precepts of the Law.

THE DISORDER OF COVETOUS DESIRES - The sensitive appetite leads us to desire pleasant things we do not have, e.g., the desire to eat when we are hungry or to warm ourselves when we are cold. These desires are good in themselves, but often they exceed the limits of reason and drive us to covet unjustly what is not ours and belongs to another or is owed to him. The Tenth Commandment forbids greed and the desire to amass earthly goods without limit. It forbids avarice arising from a passion for riches and their attendant power. It also forbids the desire to commit injustice by harming our neighbor in his temporal goods: When the Law says, "You shall not covet," these words mean that we should banish our desires for whatever does not belong to us. Our thirst for another's goods is immense, infinite, never quenched. Thus, it is written: "He who loves money never has money enough." It is not a violation of this Commandment to desire to obtain things that belong to one's neighbor, provided this is done by just means. Traditional catechesis realistically mentions "those who have a harder struggle against their criminal desires" and so who "must be urged the more to keep this commandment," merchants who desire scarcity and rising prices, who cannot bear not to be the only ones buying and selling so that they themselves can sell more dearly and buy more cheaply; those who hope that their peers will be impoverished, in order to realize a profit either by selling to them or buying from them . . . physicians who wish disease to spread; lawyers who are eager for many important cases and trials.

The Tenth Commandment requires that envy be banished from the human heart. When the prophet Nathan wanted to spur King David to repentance, he told him the story about the poor man who had only one ewe lamb that he treated like his own daughter and the rich man who, despite the great number of his flocks, envied the poor man and ended by stealing his lamb. Envy can lead to the worst crimes. "Through the devil's envy death entered the world": We fight one another, and envy arms us against one another. . . . If everyone strives to unsettle the Body of Christ, where shall we end up? We are engaged in making Christ's Body a corpse. . . . We declare ourselves members of one and the same organism, yet we devour one another like beasts.

Envy is a capital sin. It refers to the sadness at the sight of another's goods and the immoderate desire to acquire them for oneself, even unjustly. When it wishes grave harm to a neighbor it is a mortal sin: St. Augustine saw envy as "the diabolical sin." "From envy are born hatred, detraction, calumny, joy caused by the misfortune of a neighbor, and displeasure caused by his prosperity." Envy represents a form of sadness and therefore a refusal of charity; the baptized person should struggle against it by exercising good will. Envy often comes from pride; the baptized person should train himself to live in humility: Would you like to see God glorified by you? Then rejoice in your brother's progress and you will immediately give glory to God. Because his servant could conquer envy by rejoicing in the merits of others, God will be praised.

POVERTY OF HEART - Jesus enjoins his disciples to prefer him to everything and everyone, and bids them "renounce all that [they have]" for his sake and that of the gospel. Shortly before his passion he gave them the example of the poor widow of Jerusalem who, out of her poverty, gave all that she had to live on. The precept of detachment from riches is obligatory for entrance into the Kingdom of heaven.

100 days to Freedom

Day 100

Living the Freedom

Congratulations, you have completed something that 99% of humanity will never have the opportunity or stamina to complete. Congratulations. This has not been an easy task.

Now we must give some consideration to where do we go from here? What do we do now that we have finished the 100 days? Well, first of all, we should prayerfully discern what elements of the program were the most beneficial and if there is something that could be continued on a long-term basis either in its fullness or in a reduced form. Then we need to consider what it is that we still need to work on.

At the core of our lives is our need to communicate with God and to create environments that are conducive to allowing a spiritual connection. Here are some things to consider taken from an article titled *5 ways to live like a monk without actually being one* by Fr. Paul Sheller, OSB, Vocation Director, Conception Abbey.

1. **Cultivate Silence** - St. Benedict wrote, "Speaking and teaching are the master's task; the disciple is to be silent and listen" (RB 6:8). Silence is the environment that allows you to listen to God's voice and the voices of those around you properly. Many people are uncomfortable with silence or they find it awkward, so they fill their days with needless noise and distractions. Turning off the music and radio, especially when you are in the car, moderating television or Internet use will challenge you to listen to the God who dwells within you and speaks in the depth of your heart. Additionally, being silent helps us to avoid the sins of gossip or detraction. St. Benedict echoed the wisdom found in the Book of Proverbs which says, "In a flood of words you will not avoid sin," (RB 6:11). By avoiding unnecessary noise in your life, you learn to cultivate inner silence, which is the ideal setting for prayer.

2. Be Faithful to Daily Prayer - St. Benedict said, "Prayer should, therefore, be short and pure, unless perhaps it is prolonged under the inspiration of divine grace" (RB 20:4). This instruction is comforting for those who have a demanding work week, hectic schedule, and are burdened with numerous responsibilities at home to the extent that they may not be able to dedicate large periods of time to prayer. Nevertheless, you should find time in the morning to praise God before your day begins, and pray in thanksgiving during the evening before going to bed. You can pray the Liturgy of the Hours to sanctify the day, specifically being faithful to Morning and Evening Prayer. Whatever your practice, you want to be concerned with developing a heartfelt attitude to God while you are praying, offering yourself and your loved ones into God's care. Many opportunities will arise throughout the day to offer brief prayers of trust in God. The aim of monks (and all Christians) is to pray without ceasing, and you can do this by keeping the memory of God alive in your heart and mind at every moment.

3. Form Authentic Community - Monks support and encourage the brother encountering difficulties, and they celebrate with one another during joyful times. St. Benedict instructed, "No one is to pursue what he judges better for himself, but instead, what he judges better for someone else. To their fellow monks, they show the pure love of brothers" (RB 72:7-8). In a world of individualism, social media and superficial relationships, all people long for a deep sense of belonging and communion with one another. The spiritual life is always a journey that we undertake with others. You have to be willing to invest the time and energy to engage personally with other people and show interest in their lives, allowing your conversations to pass from surface level topics to the more meaningful areas of life. You may wish to gather with others who share your faith, values, and desire for God. Praying together, reading and discussing a spiritual book and Bible studies are all ways of coming together to grow in faith.

4. Make time for Lectio Divina - The ancient monastic practice of Lectio Divina or "sacred reading" emphasizes a slow, prayerful reading of Sacred Scripture that is intended to allow you to listen to the Word and seek peace in God's presence. St. Benedict warned his monks, "Idleness is the enemy of the soul. Therefore, the brothers should have specified periods for manual labor as well as for prayerful reading" (RB 48:1). Reflection on the Word of God, if done intensely and prayerfully, has the power of calling you to a continual conversion of life. Familiarize yourself with the method and take between 15-30 minutes a day in a quiet environment to practice Lectio Divina with Scripture or prayerfully read from the writings of the saints or other great spiritual works. Spiritual reading nourishes your mind and soul and often provides those inspired words that you needed to hear. Encountering the Word of God each day in a prayerful manner draws us into deeper communion with the One who speaks the word to us.

5. Practice Humility - Numerous parts of the Rule of St. Benedict highlight the importance of humility, most notably in Chapter 7 where St. Benedict depicts humility as a ladder with twelve rungs which the monk is to ascend. The first step is that a monk keeps the "fear of God" always before his eyes (RB 7:10). When you fear God or are in "awe" of God, you maintain a right relationship, realizing that you are a creature and not God. Humility is a virtue that needs to be developed, and it entails being down to earth, honest, and truthful, both in prayer, at work, and in everyday matters. St. Benedict wrote, "Place your hope in God alone. If you notice something good in yourself, give credit to God, not to yourself, but be certain that the evil you commit is always your own and yours to acknowledge" (RB 4:41-43). Being a humble person means being grateful for the blessings and opportunities that God gives you and recognizing that your gifts and talents have God as their source. Allow daily struggles, and even falling into sin, to be an invitation to humility, where you admit without hesitation that you must depend entirely on God's grace, and not on your strength.

* RB – Rule of Saint Benedict

Appendix

100 days to Freedom

100 Days to Freedom	Sun	Mon	Tue	Wed	Thu	Fri	Sat
Daily Mass or Daily Readings and Spiritual Communion							
Daily Rosary							
Nightly Examination of Conscience							
Daily Spiritual Reading							
Weekly Adoration							
Monthly Confession							
Exercise - Walk / Run Daily							
Exercise – Push-ups / Sit-ups/ Lunges Daily							
Exercise – Stretches Daily							
Fasting	■		■		■		■
No eating between meals, No Alcohol, No Candy / Desserts, No Fast-food, No Major Purchase, No TV or Movies, No Social Media							

Spiritual Communion

My Jesus,
I believe that you are present in the Most Holy Sacrament. I love you above all things, and I desire to receive You into my soul. Since I cannot at this moment receive You Sacramentally, come at least spiritually into my heart. I embrace You as if You were already there and unite myself wholly to You. Never permit me to be separated from You.

100 Days to Freedom	Sun	Mon	Tue	Wed	Thu	Fri	Sat
Daily Mass or Daily Readings and Spiritual Communion							
Daily Rosary							
Nightly Examination of Conscience							
Daily Spiritual Reading							
Weekly Adoration							
Monthly Confession							
Exercise - Walk / Run Daily							
Exercise – Push-ups / Sit-ups/ Lunges Daily							
Exercise – Stretches Daily							
Fasting	■		■		■		■
No eating between meals, No Alcohol, No Candy / Desserts, No Fast-food, No Major Purchase, No TV or Movies, No Social Media							

Spiritual Communion

My Jesus,
I believe that you are present in the Most Holy Sacrament. I love you above all things, and I desire to receive You into my soul. Since I cannot at this moment receive You Sacramentally, come at least spiritually into my heart. I embrace You as if You were already there and unite myself wholly to You. Never permit me to be separated from You.

100 Days to Freedom	Sun	Mon	Tue	Wed	Thu	Fri	Sat
Daily Mass or Daily Readings and Spiritual Communion							
Daily Rosary							
Nightly Examination of Conscience							
Daily Spiritual Reading							
Weekly Adoration							
Monthly Confession							
Exercise - Walk / Run Daily							
Exercise – Push-ups / Sit-ups/ Lunges Daily							
Exercise – Stretches Daily							
Fasting	■		■		■		■
No eating between meals, No Alcohol, No Candy / Desserts, No Fast-food, No Major Purchase, No TV or Movies, No Social Media							

Spiritual Communion

My Jesus,
I believe that you are present in the Most Holy Sacrament. I love you above all things, and I desire to receive You into my soul. Since I cannot at this moment receive You Sacramentally, come at least spiritually into my heart. I embrace You as if You were already there and unite myself wholly to You. Never permit me to be separated from You.

100 days to Freedom

100 Days to Freedom	Sun	Mon	Tue	Wed	Thu	Fri	Sat
Daily Mass or Daily Readings and Spiritual Communion							
Daily Rosary							
Nightly Examination of Conscience							
Daily Spiritual Reading							
Weekly Adoration							
Monthly Confession							
Exercise - Walk / Run Daily							
Exercise – Push-ups / Sit-ups/ Lunges Daily							
Exercise – Stretches Daily							
Fasting	■		■		■		■
No eating between meals, No Alcohol, No Candy / Desserts, No Fast-food, No Major Purchase, No TV or Movies, No Social Media							

Spiritual Communion

My Jesus,
I believe that you are present in the Most Holy Sacrament. I love you above all things, and I desire to receive You into my soul. Since I cannot at this moment receive You Sacramentally, come at least spiritually into my heart. I embrace You as if You were already there and unite myself wholly to You. Never permit me to be separated from You.

100 Days to Freedom	Sun	Mon	Tue	Wed	Thu	Fri	Sat
Daily Mass or Daily Readings and Spiritual Communion							
Daily Rosary							
Nightly Examination of Conscience							
Daily Spiritual Reading							
Weekly Adoration							
Monthly Confession							
Exercise - Walk / Run Daily							
Exercise – Push-ups / Sit-ups/ Lunges Daily							
Exercise – Stretches Daily							
Fasting	■		■		■		■
No eating between meals, No Alcohol, No Candy / Desserts, No Fast-food, No Major Purchase, No TV or Movies, No Social Media							

Spiritual Communion

My Jesus,
I believe that you are present in the Most Holy Sacrament. I love you above all things, and I desire to receive You into my soul. Since I cannot at this moment receive You Sacramentally, come at least spiritually into my heart. I embrace You as if You were already there and unite myself wholly to You. Never permit me to be separated from You.

100 Days to Freedom	Sun	Mon	Tue	Wed	Thu	Fri	Sat
Daily Mass or Daily Readings and Spiritual Communion							
Daily Rosary							
Nightly Examination of Conscience							
Daily Spiritual Reading							
Weekly Adoration							
Monthly Confession							
Exercise - Walk / Run Daily							
Exercise – Push-ups / Sit-ups/ Lunges Daily							
Exercise – Stretches Daily							
Fasting	■		■		■		■
No eating between meals, No Alcohol, No Candy / Desserts, No Fast-food, No Major Purchase, No TV or Movies, No Social Media							

Spiritual Communion

My Jesus,
I believe that you are present in the Most Holy Sacrament. I love you above all things, and I desire to receive You into my soul. Since I cannot at this moment receive You Sacramentally, come at least spiritually into my heart. I embrace You as if You were already there and unite myself wholly to You. Never permit me to be separated from You.

100 days to Freedom

100 Days to Freedom	Sun	Mon	Tue	Wed	Thu	Fri	Sat
Daily Mass or Daily Readings and Spiritual Communion							
Daily Rosary							
Nightly Examination of Conscience							
Daily Spiritual Reading							
Weekly Adoration							
Monthly Confession							
Exercise - Walk / Run Daily							
Exercise – Push-ups / Sit-ups/ Lunges Daily							
Exercise – Stretches Daily							
Fasting	■		■		■		■

No eating between meals, No Alcohol, No Candy / Desserts, No Fast-food, No Major Purchase, No TV or Movies, No Social Media

Spiritual Communion

My Jesus,
I believe that you are present in the Most Holy Sacrament. I love you above all things, and I desire to receive You into my soul. Since I cannot at this moment receive You Sacramentally, come at least spiritually into my heart. I embrace You as if You were already there and unite myself wholly to You. Never permit me to be separated from You.

100 Days to Freedom	Sun	Mon	Tue	Wed	Thu	Fri	Sat
Daily Mass or Daily Readings and Spiritual Communion							
Daily Rosary							
Nightly Examination of Conscience							
Daily Spiritual Reading							
Weekly Adoration							
Monthly Confession							
Exercise - Walk / Run Daily							
Exercise – Push-ups / Sit-ups/ Lunges Daily							
Exercise – Stretches Daily							
Fasting	■		■		■		■

No eating between meals, No Alcohol, No Candy / Desserts, No Fast-food, No Major Purchase, No TV or Movies, No Social Media

Spiritual Communion

My Jesus,
I believe that you are present in the Most Holy Sacrament. I love you above all things, and I desire to receive You into my soul. Since I cannot at this moment receive You Sacramentally, come at least spiritually into my heart. I embrace You as if You were already there and unite myself wholly to You. Never permit me to be separated from You.

100 Days to Freedom	Sun	Mon	Tue	Wed	Thu	Fri	Sat
Daily Mass or Daily Readings and Spiritual Communion							
Daily Rosary							
Nightly Examination of Conscience							
Daily Spiritual Reading							
Weekly Adoration							
Monthly Confession							
Exercise - Walk / Run Daily							
Exercise – Push-ups / Sit-ups/ Lunges Daily							
Exercise – Stretches Daily							
Fasting	■		■		■		■

No eating between meals, No Alcohol, No Candy / Desserts, No Fast-food, No Major Purchase, No TV or Movies, No Social Media

Spiritual Communion

My Jesus,
I believe that you are present in the Most Holy Sacrament. I love you above all things, and I desire to receive You into my soul. Since I cannot at this moment receive You Sacramentally, come at least spiritually into my heart. I embrace You as if You were already there and unite myself wholly to You. Never permit me to be separated from You.

100 days to Freedom

100 Days to Freedom	Sun	Mon	Tue	Wed	Thu	Fri	Sat
Daily Mass or Daily Readings and Spiritual Communion							
Daily Rosary							
Nightly Examination of Conscience							
Daily Spiritual Reading							
Weekly Adoration							
Monthly Confession							
Exercise - Walk / Run Daily							
Exercise – Push-ups / Sit-ups / Lunges Daily							
Exercise – Stretches Daily							
Fasting	■		■		■		■
No eating between meals, No Alcohol, No Candy / Desserts, No Fast-food, No Major Purchase, No TV or Movies, No Social Media							

Spiritual Communion

My Jesus,
I believe that you are present in the Most Holy Sacrament. I love you above all things, and I desire to receive You into my soul. Since I cannot at this moment receive You Sacramentally, come at least spiritually into my heart. I embrace You as if You were already there and unite myself wholly to You. Never permit me to be separated from You.

100 Days to Freedom	Sun	Mon	Tue	Wed	Thu	Fri	Sat
Daily Mass or Daily Readings and Spiritual Communion							
Daily Rosary							
Nightly Examination of Conscience							
Daily Spiritual Reading							
Weekly Adoration							
Monthly Confession							
Exercise - Walk / Run Daily							
Exercise – Push-ups / Sit-ups / Lunges Daily							
Exercise – Stretches Daily							
Fasting	■		■		■		■
No eating between meals, No Alcohol, No Candy / Desserts, No Fast-food, No Major Purchase, No TV or Movies, No Social Media							

Spiritual Communion

My Jesus,
I believe that you are present in the Most Holy Sacrament. I love you above all things, and I desire to receive You into my soul. Since I cannot at this moment receive You Sacramentally, come at least spiritually into my heart. I embrace You as if You were already there and unite myself wholly to You. Never permit me to be separated from You.

100 Days to Freedom	Sun	Mon	Tue	Wed	Thu	Fri	Sat
Daily Mass or Daily Readings and Spiritual Communion							
Daily Rosary							
Nightly Examination of Conscience							
Daily Spiritual Reading							
Weekly Adoration							
Monthly Confession							
Exercise - Walk / Run Daily							
Exercise – Push-ups / Sit-ups / Lunges Daily							
Exercise – Stretches Daily							
Fasting	■		■		■		■
No eating between meals, No Alcohol, No Candy / Desserts, No Fast-food, No Major Purchase, No TV or Movies, No Social Media							

Spiritual Communion

My Jesus,
I believe that you are present in the Most Holy Sacrament. I love you above all things, and I desire to receive You into my soul. Since I cannot at this moment receive You Sacramentally, come at least spiritually into my heart. I embrace You as if You were already there and unite myself wholly to You. Never permit me to be separated from You.

100 days to Freedom

100 Days to Freedom	Sun	Mon	Tue	Wed	Thu	Fri	Sat
Daily Mass or Daily Readings and Spiritual Communion							
Daily Rosary							
Nightly Examination of Conscience							
Daily Spiritual Reading							
Weekly Adoration							
Monthly Confession							
Exercise - Walk / Run Daily							
Exercise – Push-ups / Sit-ups/ Lunges Daily							
Exercise – Stretches Daily							
Fasting		■		■		■	
No eating between meals, No Alcohol, No Candy / Desserts, No Fast-food, No Major Purchase, No TV or Movies, No Social Media							

Spiritual Communion

My Jesus,
I believe that you are present in the Most Holy Sacrament. I love you above all things, and I desire to receive You into my soul. Since I cannot at this moment receive You Sacramentally, come at least spiritually into my heart. I embrace You as if You were already there and unite myself wholly to You. Never permit me to be separated from You.

100 Days to Freedom	Sun	Mon	Tue	Wed	Thu	Fri	Sat
Daily Mass or Daily Readings and Spiritual Communion							
Daily Rosary							
Nightly Examination of Conscience							
Daily Spiritual Reading							
Weekly Adoration							
Monthly Confession							
Exercise - Walk / Run Daily							
Exercise – Push-ups / Sit-ups/ Lunges Daily							
Exercise – Stretches Daily							
Fasting	■		■		■		■
No eating between meals, No Alcohol, No Candy / Desserts, No Fast-food, No Major Purchase, No TV or Movies, No Social Media							

Spiritual Communion

My Jesus,
I believe that you are present in the Most Holy Sacrament. I love you above all things, and I desire to receive You into my soul. Since I cannot at this moment receive You Sacramentally, come at least spiritually into my heart. I embrace You as if You were already there and unite myself wholly to You. Never permit me to be separated from You.

100 Days to Freedom	Sun	Mon	Tue	Wed	Thu	Fri	Sat
Daily Mass or Daily Readings and Spiritual Communion							
Daily Rosary							
Nightly Examination of Conscience							
Daily Spiritual Reading							
Weekly Adoration							
Monthly Confession							
Exercise - Walk / Run Daily							
Exercise – Push-ups / Sit-ups/ Lunges Daily							
Exercise – Stretches Daily							
Fasting	■		■		■		■
No eating between meals, No Alcohol, No Candy / Desserts, No Fast-food, No Major Purchase, No TV or Movies, No Social Media							

Spiritual Communion

My Jesus,
I believe that you are present in the Most Holy Sacrament. I love you above all things, and I desire to receive You into my soul. Since I cannot at this moment receive You Sacramentally, come at least spiritually into my heart. I embrace You as if You were already there and unite myself wholly to You. Never permit me to be separated from You.

About the Author

Deacon Pat Kearns lives with his wife, Liz, in Northern California. They have three grown children. Deacon Pat is a U.S. Navy/Marine veteran, an ordained Catholic cleric, and a psychiatric nurse. He holds a master's degree in nursing leadership and management, is board certified in psychiatric and mental health nursing, and is a certified public health nurse. He is currently the Nursing Director of a large psychiatric hospital in Northern California that serves children, adolescents, and adults, and also ministers in the Sacramento diocese. He is the founder of the Family Mission Project, Catholic *Men-In-Motion* retreats, and The Catholic Journey Podcast.

Deacon Pat and Liz have also lived in Southern California, Western Idaho, and the mountains of Guatemala while serving as full-time Catholic missionaries where they developed nutritional and health care programs for the local Mayan people. Deacon Pat walked the Camino de Santiago (The Way of Saint James) across Northern Spain during the summer of 2017 with his brother Tim (one of the six brothers) and is planning to walk a similar journey across Italy in 2021.

As an author of numerous novels, spiritual guides, and bilingual children's books, Deacon Pat uses his life experiences, as well as his imagination, to create wonderful stories grounded in the faith. He has become a popular novelist due to his easy-to-read writing style, thrilling adventures, relatable and life-like characters, and also for the messages of hope, redemption, love, forgiveness, and joy that so many of the stories possess. He is also a spiritual director, gifted preacher, and a popular spiritual retreat leader.

Books by Deacon Pat Kearns
Available through Amazon.com and other outlets.

Adventure / Spiritual Novels

Forgotten & Lost

Climbing Out of the Darkness

Breaking Away

C.S.F. Catholic Special Forces

The Hermit's Word

The Hidden Journey

Church – More Than Just a Building

Spiritual Guides

100 days to Freedom

Health, Happiness, and Holiness

Children's' Books
(Bilingual - Spanish/English)

I am Nene - Yo Soy Nene

I am Isabelita - Yo Soy Isabelita

**My Greatest Treasure
"The Kearns Family"**

**Saint Patrick,
Pray for Us!**

Made in the USA
San Bernardino, CA
21 January 2020